Whitley Stokes

Some Remarks on the Celtic Additions to Curtius' Greek Etymology

Whitley Stokes

Some Remarks on the Celtic Additions to Curtius' Greek Etymology

ISBN/EAN: 9783337298050

Printed in Europe, USA, Canada, Australia, Japan

Cover: Foto ©ninafisch / pixelio.de

More available books at **www.hansebooks.com**

SOME REMARKS

ON

THE CELTIC ADDITIONS

TO

CURTIUS' *GREEK ETYMOLOGY.*

BY

WHITLEY STOKES,

VICE-PRESIDENT OF THE PHILOLOGICAL SOCIETY,
AND
HONORARY MEMBER OF THE GERMAN ORIENTAL SOCIETY.

ON THE CELTIC ADDITIONS TO CURTIUS' *GREEK ETYMOLOGY* [a].

WHILE reading the additions made by Professor Windisch to Curtius' famous book, Plato's epigram has often sounded through my brain :—

'Αστὴρ πρὶν μὲν ἔλαμπες ἐνὶ ζωοῖσιν 'Εῷος,
Νῦν δὲ θανὼν λάμπεις 'Εσπερος ἐν φθιμένοις.

For here the young scholar, already renowned as a Sanskritist, has left the East for a time, and re-appeared, a veritable Hesperos, among the dead or dying languages of the Celt. Only, thank God, the ' θανὼν ' is inapplicable, for Windisch has a long life of happy and useful activity before him. Curtius is indeed to be congratulated on having secured the aid of a linguist who has not only been trained in the best school of the new philology, but has also mastered the *Grammatica Celtica*, worked at the Dublin MSS., and thus gained a considerable knowledge of Old-Irish,—the Gothic (as Schleicher called it) of the Celtic family of speech. How excellent a recruit the little band of Celtic scholars has obtained in Windisch may be seen from his review of Fick's *Wörterbuch* in Kuhn's *Zeitschrift* xxi, from his comparisons in Curtius' book of Ir. *cruaid, cobeden, comdiu, -dia* for *dés* = δείξει, and *máo*, and from the caution and judgment which his work almost invariably displays. It is to be regretted that Windisch has not yet made thorough studies of the British languages ; for in the preservation of initial *y*, and the treatment of the combinations TN, NT, KS, SV, they stand on a higher level than the very oldest Irish ; while their regular mode of dealing with the diphthongs *ai* and *oi*, with vowel-flanked *c, g, t* and *d* in anlaut and inlaut, with *cc, tt*, and *pp*, with the combination *sp* in anlaut and the combinations *dv, rv, lv* in auslaut, often throws valuable lights on the primeval form of Celtic words. Had Windisch, for instance, remembered the British forms corresponding with the Irish *teg* (τέγος), *tech*, he would never have doubted (No. 155) that the *ch* of *tech* (τέγος) is the representative (*vertreter*) of infected *g*. Had he known that Modern Welsh *dd* invariably represents an Old-Celtic *D*, that Modern Welsh *D* between vowels invariably represents a primeval *T*, he would not have confused, as he has done in No. 635, the derivatives from an Old-Celtic root ending in D (BAD ex GVADH, whence Ir. *bádud* ' mergere,' W. *boddi*, i. e. *bodhi*, Bret. *beuziff*) with those from a root ending in T,—BHAT (Ir. *báth* ' sea,' *baithis* ' baptism,' O.W. *betid* now *bedydd*, Br. *badez* : cf. O.N. *badh*,

[a] Grundzüge der Griechischen Etymologie von Georg Curtius. Vierte durch vergleichungen aus den keltischen sprachen von Ernst Windisch erweiterte auflage. Leipzig, 1873.

A.S. *bädh*, Eng. *bath*),—and then added to these Celtic vocables the loanword *baitsim* (from *baptizo*), O.Ir. *baitzimm* (*baitzis-i* 'baptizavit cum,' Goidel^c. 87). What I have here to say may be conveniently arranged under three heads. First, I shall point out the few other errors into which (as seems to me) Windisch has fallen. Secondly, I shall mention certain words and forms which he appears to have overlooked, and which may with advantage be placed under one or other of the 664 Numbers into which the bulk of Curtius' work is now divided. Lastly, I shall notice a few of the Greek words which Curtius has omitted, but which have their cognates in the Celtic languages, and may, therefore, deserve to be dealt with in a book intended not merely for classical students, but also for all comparative philologists.

I.—CORRIGENDA.

First of all, on behalf of sound philology, I must protest against the use of O'Reilly's dictionary for scientific purposes. The book is quite untrustworthy : it swarms with forgeries and blunders : and its only value lies in the extracts which it contains from O'Clery and other old glossarists, whose explanations O'Reilly often misunderstands. Yet from this polluted source Windisch takes at No. 8 *art* ª 'bear ;' at No. 54 *capat ;* at No. 302 *aidhe* 'house' (a blunder for *aicde*) ; at No. 411 *bar* 'getreide ;' at No. 528 *duad* 'toil ;' at No. 543 *leon, leoghan* 'lion.' It is to be hoped that these figments will be expunged from the next edition of Curtius' book. So, at No. 68 Windisch should not have cited Mr. Crowe's *celt* 'hair.' Windisch was long enough in Ireland to learn that certain self-styled Irish scholars are like some of the Paṇḍits here in India, able to produce any word for any meaning, and any meaning for any word ᵇ. *Celt* (anglicised *kilt*) means 'vestis' according to Cormac : (so O'Clery : *realt* .i. *édach*), and belongs to *celare* and other words noticed at No. 30. In the passage referred to by Mr. Crowe (*issed étach fil impu celt asas tréu*, LU. 95b, the author uses *celt* to denote 'hair' just as Lucretius, v. 672, uses *vestis* to denote the beard as the *covering* of the chin.

ª Forged in imitation of the Welsh *arth*, just as O'Reilly has *sciberneog* 'hare' and *cae* 'hedge,' counterfeits of Welsh *ysgyfarnog* and *cae*.
ᵇ Take a few examples from Mr. Crowe's *Scéla na Esérgi*, Dublin, 1865 :—

    p. 6, l. 23, *rotomlithe* ' they were drowned' (*rectè* 'they were devoured ').
    p. 12, *is[s]ochma* 'it is easy' (*rectè* ' there is power ').
    p. 12, *todochaide* ' expectation ' (*rectè* ' future ').
    p. 18, *hetar* ' is possible ' (*rectè* ' is found ').
    p. 20, *lucht ind remeca* ' the previsionists ' (*rectè* ' they who die prematurely ').
    p. 22, *diafil in forbairt* ' which goes to decay ' (*rectè* 'which has the increase ').
    p. 24, *atchichestar* ' shall be worshipped (?) ' (*rectè* 'shall he seen ').
Take a few from his *Amra Choluim Chille* (Dublin, 1873) :—
    p. 12, *achubus cox : a anim glan* 'O tree of bounds : O pure soul !' (*rectè* ' O fair conscience ! O pure soul !').
    dochendnaib 'of headlets' (*rectè* ' extempore ').
    p. 16, *águr* ' I ask ' (*rectè* ' I fear ').
    p. 26, *cen cholt ar cráib cernine* 'without fruit on branch of *cernine*' (*rectè* ' without food quickly on a dish ').
    p. 34, *accestar* ' he saw ' (*rectè* 'is seen ').
    p. 44, *gair arrith* ' Cry is attacking' (*rectè* ' short is her course ').
    p. 46, *atbeir cet* 'prophecy says' (*rectè* 'who says *cet*, i. e. permission ').
    p. 52, *nodgeilsigfe* ' has associated him ' (*rectè* ' will take him into household ').
It is time to notice Mr. Crowe's mistranslations when, like dirt, they are ' matter in the wrong place.'

At Nos. 129 and 443 Windisch's trustfulness in a dangerous guide has again misled him. At No. 129 he cites as cognate with γέρανος, *grus*, etc. 'altir. (*grén* ?), gen. *griúin*,' and refers to a quotation from Lebor na huidre, describing Cúchulainn's seven fingers, *con-gabáil ingne sebaic, co-forgabail ingne griúin*, which Mr. Crowe translates 'with the catch of the talons of a hawk, with the detention of the talons of a crane;' but which means, I think, 'with the grasp of a hawk's talons, with the clutch of a griffon's (?) claws.' Whatever *griúin* may mean [a], it cannot be 'crane,' for a crane has blunt-nailed toes, which have no power of grasping or 'detention.' At No. 443, Windisch renders *ro-snaidet* by 'sie schwimmen stark.' This is a literal rendering of Mr. Crowe's absurd 'they strong-swim;' but *ro-snaidet* is a preterito-present (Beitr. vii. 3) and simply means 'they swam.'

At No. 166 Windisch has been misled by Zeuss: *ocht* (leg. *ócht*) means 'frigus,' not 'angustia.' It occurs (spelt *uacht*) in Fiacc's hymn, l. 27, and is now *f-uacht* with prosthetic *f*. In Z. 1006 *ócht* is misrendered by 'necessitate' and *ocht* (leg. *ócht*) by 'angustia.' In the former case substitute 'frigore,' in the latter 'frigus.' The Irish cognate of *angustia*, ἄχος, etc. is *ochte*, a feminine *ā*-stem, which occurs in Z. 68.

No. 190. Windisch puts Irish *géd* (W. *gwydd* f., Corn. *guith*, Br. *goaz*) with χήν from χένς; he has not, however, explained how this is possible. *Géd* and the British words above quoted come from *gédā, *gēndā, gendā* (the Teutonic *ganta* [b]), just as W. *ysgwydd* 'shoulder' f., Corn. *scuid*, Br. *scoaz*, come from *scēdā, *scēndā, *scendā* (the Skr. *skandha*): cf. the Latin *mētior*, *vēsica* (from *mentior, vensica*), the Gr. μήδεα, ἤδομαι, and other examples cited by Schmidt *zur geschichte des indogerm. vocalismus*, 118, 120.

No. 194. There is no such Irish word as *gaim* 'winter,' although this form is found in the place whence Windisch takes it. It is a scribe's mistake for *gam*, O'Clery's *gamh* .i. *geimhreadh*. The British forms have a diphthong, like χειμών: O.W. *gaem*, Z. 104, Corn. *goyf*, Br. *gouaff*.

No. 205. The Cymric '*stirenn*,' here cited from Ebel's Zeuss, p. 120, is non-existent. The MS. (which, by-the-way, is Old-Cornish, not Cymric) has *scirenn* (W. *ysgyren*), Z. 1063, and the Mediæval Latin *stella* which it glosses does not mean 'star,' but 'splint,' the French '*estelle* de bois.' *Scirenn*, Corn. *skyrenn* (pl. *skyrennou*, B.M. 3403), M.Br. *squezrenn* (leg. *squerenn* [c]), appear connected with σκύλοψ, *qui-squiliæ*, Curtius No. 114. So perhaps Ir. *scol-b* (*scolb tige*), gl. tegulus, Ir. Gl. No. 446).

No. 238. Here are two strange mistakes: First, *tair* 'come' has nothing to do with the root TAR. It is the 2d sg. *s*-conjunctive (here used as an imperative) of a verb of which *tairic* (= *do-air-IC*) .i. *tig* 'venit,' O'Cl., is the 3d sg. present. No Irish word can end in *rs*, and *tair* stands for *tairs, *do-air-s, do-air-IC-s,

---

[a] O'Clery explains *criun* by *mac tíre* 'wolf' and *griun* by *graineog* 'hedgehog.' Neither meaning suits here.

[b] (anseres) e Germaniâ laudatissimi. Candidi ibi, verum minores *gantæ* vocantur, Plin. 10, 22, 27, cited in Smith's Latin Dictionary. Cf. OHG. *ganzo*, A.S. *gandra*, Eng. *gander*, A.S. *ganot, ganet*, Eng. *gannet* 'fulica.'

[c] *zl, zr* for *l, r* are often found in M.Bret.: cf. *bouhazl* 'securis,' *bouclezr* 'bouclier,' etc.

just as *coméir*, the 2d sg. *s*-conj. of *comérgim*, stands for **coméirs ;* but the *s* is found in the 3d pl. *tairset* (do-air-IC-sent) 'veniant,' Colm. H. 45, and the 1st pl. *comairsem* (*com-air*-IC-*semm*) 'attingemus,' Z. 467. The *s* is also lost in the 3d sg. *do-mm-air* 'veniat mihi,' *con-om-thair* 'ut mihi veniat,' *ni-m-thair* ' ne mihi veniat,' Z. 466. The root is ANK, and *tair* belongs to No. 424, not to No. 238. The second mistake is citing the non-existent *imthirid :* the word meant is *timthirthid* (do-imb-tar-i-titi-s) ἀμφίπολος, Beitr. vi. 471.

No. 267b. ' Ir. *druim,*' says Windisch, ' geht auf **drosomi* wie *tirim* auf **tarsimi.*' But these hypothetical forms would have given **dróimh* and **tirimh,* whereas the *m* in *druim* and *tirim* is hard [a]. *Druim* (better *druimm*), moreover, is a stem in *men* (acc. pl. *tocraid forn-drommand fri fraigid uli* ' set your backs, all of you, to the wall !' Mesca Ulad, LU. 19a). Read therefore ' *druimm* (Gen. *drommo*, acc. pl. *drommann*) geht auf **drosmen* für **dors-men.*' As to *tirim* it is probably from **tirimbi-s.*

No. 275. Here Windisch says that *daur* (gl. quercus) is for *daru ;* but it is a stem in *c* not *u* (*cnu na darach* 'nux quercus,' Z. 260) and stands for **dair(ic)*, **daric.* Before r or an infected dental, *au* is frequently written for *ai* (the infected *a*). See Zeuss 7.

No. 342. Here Windisch, misled by a printer's error in Ebel's edition of the *Gr. Celtica,* says ' *niæ* bedeutet auch soror.' The passage cited in support of this—' *im orba mic niath* '—means ' circa hereditatem filii filii sororis.' The fuller form of the word, *gnia .i. mac seathar* ' filius sororis,' is given by O'Clery, and belongs to No. 128.

No. 446. Old-Irish *ainm* is for **anme*, **anmen*, not, as Windisch writes, *anmi.* So No. 517 *sruaim,* another stem in *men* (dat. pl. *sruamannaib,* O'Dav. Gl. 117) is for **srômen* = in form Lat. *rûmen*, in meaning *Rumo*, Στρύμων.

No. 492. *Ara,* gen. *arad,* ('charioteer') cannot ever have been, as Windisch asserts, a participle present active. Had it been a participle, its gen. sg. would have been **arat*, ex **arantos.* A similar mistake is made under No. 415, in dealing with the ant-stem *tipra.*

No. 518. *Sreth* never means ' strues,' though Zeuss 992 seems to think it does. The Irish word for ' strues ' is *sreith*, and comes under No. 215.

At p. 572 a serious error has been committed. The Old-Irish *tarb, dclb, fedb* are cited as examples of the hardening of *v* to *b.* Nothing can be more certain than that here, as in *Ioib*, *breib* and *barn* ' vester,' Z. 339, as in the Hiberno-Latin *bobes* (Z. 54) *corbus*, *fubonius* (Reeves' *Columba* xviii) the *b* is a mere graphic representative of *v.* If the *b* in *tarb* were really a *b*, we should certainly have sometimes found the word written as *tarp* or *tarbb* (see Z. 60) ; but it is always *tarb* or *tarbh* in Mediæval-Irish MSS. [b] ; and we should have had *tarb* in the modern language instead of the actual *tarbh*, pronounced *tarv.* The Gaulish and Welsh forms *tarvos*, *tarw*, also speak unmistakeably for our theory.

---

[a] So in *trum*, the Modern Welsh representative of *druimm*. For Modern Welsh *tr* = Ir. *dr :* cf. *trín* ' battle' = O.Ir. *drenn, trythyll* ' voluptuous ' = O.Ir. *drettell* ' deliciæ.' See, too, Rhys, *Rev. Celtique,* i. 363.

[b] In the *Crith Gablach,* as printed in the third volume of O'Curry's *Manners and Customs of the Ancient Irish,* p. 486, l. 16, it is true that we find *tarbb ;* but in the MS. (H. 3. 18, p. 254), of which I have a photograph before me, the word in question is distinctly *tarbh*.

It will have been seen that most of these errors are due to Windisch's belief in his predecessors. *Oportet discentem credere.* But Windisch is now a teacher, not a learner, and in no department of philology is the apostolic precept *Omnia probate* more needed than in the Celtic, with its forged words, inaccurate texts, unfaithful translations, and ignorant native scholars.

II.—ADDENDA.

Let us now proceed with the second division of this Paper, namely, the further additions which, I venture to think, may be made to Curtius' work :—

No. 1, p. 130. To the root AK belongs the Old-Irish *ánne* 'ring' (now *f-áinne* with prosthetic *f*), Corm., which stands for **acn-nio* as the cognate Lat. *ánus* for **acnus.* To the nasalised form of this root, ANK, belongs the O.Ir. *æcath* for *écath* (gl. hamus) Z. 1009 = *ecad* .i. *saith ecca* .i. *biad necca* ('cibus mortis') .i. *pisci*, O'Mulc. Gl. H. 2. 16, col. 101 : the Mcd.-Br. *iguenn* 'hamus,' Cath., is from the primary form.

No. 2. Add the Old-Welsh *auc* (=āçus, ὠκύς) in *diauc* (gl. segnem), Juv. 93, Br. *di-ec* 'segnis,' 'piger:' the Welsh *egr* 'acer' = O.Ir. *aicher :* the O.Ir. verb *do-r-acráid* (gl. exacerbavit), Z. 462, *doaccradi* (gl. exasperat), Ml. 28a, Br. *diegraff* 'exacerbare,' Cath. To the extended root AKS (whence ὀξύς) the Old-Welsh *och*, Beitr. vii, 412, now *awch* 'edge,' appears to belong.

No. 4. ἀκχός. Windisch (Vorrede, p. x) has put *asil* (gl. artus) to this Number. He might also add the diminutive *aislean* (gl. articulo), Goidelᵉ. 23, and the M.Br. *asquell* 'āla' (for **axla*).

No. 13. To the root DARK 'to see' the Welsh *drych* = Br. *derch* should be referred. Siegfried's ingenious explanation of Lat. *larva* ex **dar(c)va* (as *laurus* ex **daurus*, *lacryma* ex *dacruma*) is also deserving of notice.

No. 14. O.Ir. *adéos* .i. *sloinnfed no inneosad* 'I will declare, or I will relate,' O'Cl., is for **ad-décsû*, where *décsû* = δείξω.

No. 15. The Irish *doich, doig* 'verisimilis,' Z. 74, 305, compar. *dochu*, Z. 276, certainly goes with δοκέω. Glück (Neue Jahrbücher für Philologie, 1864, s. 602) connected the Old-Celtic names *Decangi, Decanti, Decetia* with *decus, decor.* With these also goes the Irish adjective *dech, deg* used as a superlative to *maith* 'good' (*deach* .i. *feurr*, O'Cl.), *innani as-deg rochreitset hier* (gl. electorum dei) i. e. 'of those who best believed in Christ,' Z. 611, where it is wrongly explained by Zeuss.

No. 22. Ir. *faile* 'a gap' (= W. *bolch, bwlch* ?) belongs to αὖλαξ, ὁλκός, etc.

No. 28. κάκκη. Add W. *cach* m., where *ch* is from *cc*, Z. 151.

No. 29b. Ir. *cailech* 'gallus' (= **calico-s*) belongs to καλέω and the other words here cited. The Ir. *caol* .i. *cail* .i. *gairm* 'clamor,' O'Cl., the W. *ceiliog* 'gallus,' come from a by-form of the root, KIL: cf. O.N. *hjal*, OHG. *hël* (in *gi-hël*, etc.), NHG. *hell*, Fick 725.

No. 30. With the root καλ, Lat. *celare*, OHG. *hëlan*, the Welsh *celu* 'to hide,' 'to conceal,' is connected. In Irish the root is found not only in *cel-t* 'vestis,' but in the verb *fo-n-ro-chled* [a] 'occlusi sumus,' Z. 483, and the substantive *cleith* .i. *ceilt* 'concealment,' O'Cl., whence the adverb *fochleith* 'clam,' O'Don. Gr. 267, *cleth* (gl. laterna) Sg. 51b, and the following words cited by Nigra (*Reliquiæ Celticæ* i. 36n.), *clithith* (gl. latex), *inna cletha* (gl. latebras), *á-chlid* (gl. latibulum suum), *nu-da-chelat* (gl. latentes), *con-ai-celt* (gl. desimulavit), *in-chlide* (reconditæ). The Irish *cell* is a loan from *cella*, here cited, and *caille*, which Ebel, Beitr. ii. 169, connects with *celo*, etc., is certainly (like W. *pall*) a loan from *pallium*.

No. 31. The Ir. *cél*, W. *coil, coel* 'augurium' are connected by Fick with καλός, the Celtic and Northern-European forms resting on **kaila*. The Ir. *célmuine* = W. *coelfain* 'glad tidings :' *an-ceoil* .i. *uile orra* 'evils on them !' O'Cl., may also be here cited.

No. 32. W. *can, caniad* 'song,' Corn. *can*, pl. *canow*, Br. *canaff* 'chanter,' Cath., are cognate with *cano*, κανάζω. The Irish *cainte* 'satirist,' *caint* 'speech' may also be cognate, though the hard *t* is not easily explained.

No. 37. The Gaulish *gabro-s* (in *Gabro-sentum*, *Gabro-magus*, Glück, KN. 43), Ir. *gabar*, W. *gafr*, Corn. *gavar*, Br. *gaffr* 'cheure,' Cath., can hardly be separated from κάπρος, *caper*, etc. We must assume in these Celtic words an abnormal sinking of the tenues, which we also find in *gabáil* = 'capere,' κώπη No. 34, and *goirt* 'bitter' = Lith. *kartus*, Skr. kaṭu, 'sharp,' 'pungent,' and possibly also in *doich* 'swift,' *droch* 'wheel,' *infra*, at No. 178.

No. 41. O.Ir. *crip*, for **cirp*, which O'Davoren 63 and O'Clery explain by *luath* 'swift,' is almost certainly cognate with καρπ-άλιμος and κραιπνός. See further Corm. Tr. 143.

No. 42b. Ir. *cloch* 'stone' f. is = κρόκη here cited : *cora* 'stones,' Corm. Tr. 87, *cert-fuine* 'the flag on which bread is kneaded or baked,' O'Don. Supp., *calad* = *calat* (gl. durili) Z. 1064, also belong to this Number. Rhys, *Rev. Celtique* i. 364, also puts W. *corwg*, Irish *curach* 'a little boat' (cf. Lat. *carina*) and W. *caregl* with Skr. *karaka* 'cocoanut-shell' here cited. The Irish *curach* is from **curoch* = *curuca* (which actually occurs in Adamnán's Life of Columba, ed. Reeves, pp. 176,177), the sequence *u-o* becoming *u-a* as in *pudar* from *putor*, *sdupar* from *stupor*, Corm. Tr. 167.

No. 45. The Low-Latin *cayum* 'domus' (= a Gaulish *caion*), Ir. *cae* .i. *tech*, O'Curry's Transcript of Brehon Laws, p. 100, *cerdd-chae* (gl. officina, 'fabri domus'), Z. 60, is surely cognate with κοί-τη, *quies*, *hei-va* (domus) and the other words here cited. The W. *cae*= *kue* 'sæpimentum,' Z. 285, pl. *caiou* (gl. munimenta), Br. *quae* 'hayc d'espine', 'seps,' Cath., is a different word, and has perhaps lost a vowel-flanked *g* : cf. O.N. *hagi, ge-hege*.

No. 45b. Ir. *scian* 'knife,' W. *ysgien*, are certainly cognate with *de-sci-scere*, (σ)κείω. So M.Bret. *squeiaff* 'coupper,' 'amputare,' Cath. = W. *ysgiaw*. Curtius' ingenious argument, p. 109, for connecting *scio* with *de-sci-scere* is

---

[a] Fiacc's hymn, line 15, 'Robo-chobair dond-ériun tichtu patraicc forochlad' should, I now see, be rendered ' Patrick's coming was a help to Ireland, which had been shut up.' The allusion is to Galatians iii. 23 (Vulgate): 'Antequam autem venisset fides, sub lege custodiebamur, conclusi ad fidem quæ patefacienda erat.' Correct accordingly my Goidelica², 130. Other blunders in the same book are corrected at the end of this Paper.

supported by the Irish *sliucht* 'cognitio,' Z. 878, which comes from the root SLAK, whence O.Ir. *ro-se(s)laig* (cecidit) and Goth. *slahan*.

No. 46. O.Ir. *col* ' sin,' Corm., seems cognate with κηλίς, *squalor*, &c.

No. 47. O.Ir. *céle* 'socius,' W. *celydd*, seems cognate with *callis*, κέλευθος, just as O.Ir. *sétche* ' wife ' with *sét* 'via,' and Goth. *ga-sinthia* with *sinth-s*.

No. 48. O.Ir. *céle* 'servus' is cognate with κέλης, *celer, colo: bua-chail*, W. *bu-gail* = βου-κόλος.

No. 49. The Irish preposition *cen* 'sine,' Z. 655, the adjective *cenathe*, and the adverb *in-chenadid* (gl. absque), Z. 608, seem cognate with κενεός, çūnja. No relations in the British languages except possibly *kyn* in the Corn. *kyn-byk* 'a wether-goat,' Lhuyd A.B. 65c.

No. 50. κέρας. The Old-Celtic forms κάρνον (σάλπιγγα) and κάρνυξ are well established (see Diefenbach *Origg.* 280) and should here be cited.

No. 53. Ir. *ceart* .i. *beag* ' little,' O'Cl., is in form identical with *curtus*. The Br. *di-scar* ' obruere,' like Ir. *co-scéra* (destruet), tends to show that κείρω, etc., have lost initial *s*.

No. 54. κεφαλή. The Ir. *calb* .i. *cend* 'head,' Lebar Lecain Vocab. No. 149, *(im-chalb* .i. *im-chind*, Book of Leinster, 161, b. 1, *do chalbh re cloich cruideata* .i. *do cheann re cloich chriadh nó chruaidh*, O'Cl., s. v. *Cruideata)* seems, if we assume the ordinary metathesis of a liquid, identical with the κίβλη of Callimachus.

No. 57. The Corn. *ke* 'i,' pl. *kewgh* 'ite,' the M.Br. *quæ*, now *ké*, pl. *kit*, come certainly from the root KI, whence κίω, *cio*, etc. The Irish cognates seem to be *cái* .i. *slighe no conair* 'a road or a path,' O'Cl., *cian* ' remotus,' *cein* ' time,' *cach 'la céin* ... *in-céin n-aili* 'modo ... modo,' Z. 360 : cf. the Teutonic *tid, zeit, timi, tima* from the root *di*, in Skr. *diyate, dediya*, δίεμαι.

No. 59. Welsh *clo* 'lock,' *cloig* 'hasp,' should be put with *clavis* and the other words here cited.

No. 60. O.Ir. *cloen, clóin* 'iniquus,' Z. 31, *clóine* 'iniquitas' Z. 1007, is cognate with *clino*, κλίνω and other derivatives from the root KLI.

No. 62. Ir. *cloth* = κλυτός and W. *clod* ' praise ' might also be added : *'la cluaissn'* (sic !),—cited here from Mr. Crowe's inaccurate [a] edition of the

---

[a] This is too indulgent an epithet. Consider the following *(pauca de plurimis)*:—
p. 136, *finda bi-derga* ' white-eared' *(rectè* ' white, red-eared ').
p. 138, *bes sáiniu* ' which is more distinguished ' (MS. *bess áiniu* 'which is more splendid ').
p. 140, 7 *ecrait Medb* 7 *Ailell fidchell* 'and Medb and Ailill arrange the chess-board' (MS. *Imbrid medb* 7 *ailill fidchell* ' M. and A. play chess ').
p. 140, *forri* ' on it ' (MS. *óir* ' of gold ').
p. 140, *dobor-chon* ' of water-dogs,' *(rectè* ' of otters ').
p. 144, *asbeir is corrodalldus* (MS. *asbér is cor rodalláus*).
p. 152, *immim . . . catnócaib . . . diaidsiu* (MS. *immum . . . cotnócaib . . . itladsiu*).
p. 150, *con dessar chucann* ' will be set to us ' (MS. *condessar chuca* ' will be asked of her.')
The worst of all is in p. 154, where the double diminutive *fraccnatan* 'girl ' (*frac-natan* .i. *caillin*, II. 2. 16, col. 657 : cf. *Banbnatan, Corcnatan, Becnatan*) occurs in the acc. sg. *fraccnatain*, but Mr. Crowe, not understanding this easy word, trisects it and gives us, without the slightest warning, *fracc na tain*, which he renders ' the woman of the herd.' The quotations and translations in his notes are equally valuable : *e. g.*
p. 163, *nonburn aile friu* 'another ennead [nine] by them' (MS. *nónbur naile friu anair*, LU. 94, 'another eunead to the east of them.')
p. 164, *núnbos cachu urchura* (MS. *núnbor cachu urchair*), LU. 95b.

Táin bó Fráich, is in the MS. *lacluáiss* ngléssa, the *n* of the accusative appearing only in the anlaut of the following word.

No. 63. The river-name *Clóta*, now the *Clyde*, Ir. *Cluad*, gen. *cluade* in *Ail-Cluade* 'rupes Clotæ,' (gl. on Fiacc's hymn, 1), now *Dumbarton*, is certainly connected with *cluere*, κλύ-ζω, *hlu-tr-s*. So *Glana* (pura, clara) is the name of many Celtic rivers, Glück, K.N. 187 n.

No. 64. In Kuhn's Zeitschrift xxi 429, Windisch puts Corn. *scouarn* (gl. auris) with the Hesychian (σ)κοϙ ἀκούει. The *f* in Modern Welsh *ysgyfarn* is curious. The Old-Ir. adj. *con* has been equated with the Goth. *skau-n-s schön*, here cited, just as the synonymous *cáin* ᵃ is certainly = O.S. *ski-n*, Eng. *sheen*. But the only equivalent of *con* is καινός, *καν-joς. Glück, KN. 68, puts the Irish *conn*, *cunn* 'sense,' 'understanding,' with κοννέω; but *cunn* (ex *cug-no*, as *co-vinnus* ex *covigno*) is rather to be connected with Goth. *hug-s*.

No. 65. Welsh *cwch* m. 'boat' seems cognate with κόγκος, çaṅkha. So *truch* (gl. truncate), Beitr. iv. 423, from *truncus*.

No. 66. Ir. *cuach*, W. *cóg*, Br. *coc* 'cuculus,' are all cognate with κόκκυξ, *cucŭlus*.

No. 69. The *crú* in *crú-fechta* 'corvus prælii' certainly goes with *corvus* and κόραξ. See Corm. Tr. 39, and add the following glosses : *is crú* (.i. *badb) fechta modcernæ*, LU. 109a., *crú* .i. *bodb, fechta* .i. *cath*, H. 3, 18, p. 61a.

No. 71. Curtius doubtfully places κόρδαξ with κραδάω, Skr. *kūrd*, *kūrdana*. Fick 205 also adds σκόρδαξ from Mnesimachus. The root seems to occur in Celtic : Ir. *ceird* .i. *ceimniugud no cing* 'a stepping or going,' O'Dav. 64 : *mairg misceird* ᵇ .i. *mairg dia ceimniter* (leg. *céimnigther*) *in ceird sin* 'woe to him for whom that journey is travelled,' *ib*. O.W. (Br. ?) *credam* (gl. vado) Z. 1053, for *cerdam*, Mod. W. *cerddaf* : Corn. *kerd* (gl. iter), M.Br. *querzet* 'cheminer, aler.' With Lat. *gladius* (for *cladius), Slav. *korŭda* here cited, the Irish *claid-eb*, *clainn* (= *cla-n-d-i-s), *cloinn* Corm. 'sword,' *clainneb* 'cleaver' dat. sg. *clainniub*, T. B. Fr. 142, are certainly connected.

No. 74. κρέας, *caro*. The Irish *carna* .i. *feoil* 'flesh' and *cairín* .i. *feoil gan tsaill* 'flesh without fat,' O'Cl., should be added.

No. 76. Root κρι in κρίνω, etc. Many British words belong to this Number. O.W. *cruitr* (gl. pala) Juvencus, p. 14, Corn. *croider* (gl. cribrum), whence *kroddre* 'to sift,' D. 882, Br. *croerz*, and the O.W. *cri-p* 'pecten,' Z. 1059, now *crib*, Br. *crib* 'paingne,' Cath. The ground-form of the Irish *criathar* is *crētra* (not as Windisch says, misled by me, *crētara*), Z². 166 : the second *a* is an 'irrational' vowel. The Irish *ro-scailset* here cited belongs rather to No. 664, with *scailt* 'cleft,' etc.

No. 77. κρύος. Add Corn. *kriv* (ex *crūmo-*), W. *cri* 'raw.'

No. 77b. O.Ir. *cin* 'delictum,' a *t*-stem, Z. 258, may have lost initial *s* and be cognate with A.S. *scinn-o*, *scin* 'dæmon,' 'nocivus,' Fick 201, Goth. *skātha*, Gr. κτείνω, καίνω from *σκενjω, *σκλνjω, Skr. *khata* from *skata*.

ᵃ *con-róiter* .i. *cain ro(fh)itir*, LU. Crowe's *Amra*. p. 38. *Con-fig figleastair* .i. *cain no taitnemach cach figell* 7 *cach sleachtain roflcheastair* .i. *rofuachtnaig* .i. *fria cholainn*, II. 2. 16, col. 698.

ᵇ i. e. *mis-ceird*. So *mis-imirt* .i. *droich-imirt*, O'Clery, *mis-cuis* 'odium,' Z. 864, (*cuis* = W. *cas*, Eng. *hate*). *Mis·* is of course = Goth. *missa*. *Mí* (aspirating) is perhaps = Skr. *mithu*.

No. 79. Ir. *cuach* 'beaker' = *caucus*, like κύαθος, belongs to the root κυ : also perhaps *cúana* .i. *buidhne* 'troops,' O'Cl., and *cuanna* .i. *cnoc* 'hill,' *ib.*

No. 80. Glück, KN. 28, compares Gaulish *cumba* 'convallis,' W. *cwm*, Old-French *combe* with κύμβη, κύμβος. *Cúm* 'a dell' occurs in Modern Irish topography, but seems a loan from the English *coomb*. I have never met with it in a manuscript.

No. 81. Root κυρ, κυλ. Add Br. *cor-uent* 'tourbillon.' Besides the Irish words which Windisch puts with κυλίω, κίρκος, etc., there are Ir. *cul* 'chariot,' Corm. Tr. 39, and the extended root CRID in foChRIDigedar (gl. accingit), whence *cris* 'girdle' (ex *crid-tu) Z². 954 and M.Br. *crisaff* 'succingere,' Cath. So O.Ir. *cruind (*cur-indo-s)*, Br. *crenn*. So also O.Ir. *cromb (*curumbo-s)*, W. *crom*, whence *cromman* 'sickle,' W. *cryman* 'bending,' 'curved.' That the Lat. *varus* here cited stands for *cvarus* seems doubtful from its Celtic cognates—Ir. *fiar*, W. *gwyr*, Br. *goar* in *goarec* 'arcus.'

No. 83. κυ-νέ-ω. W. *cusan* (ex *custana ?*) 'kiss' and Corn. *cussin* (gl. osculo) seem cognate with Skr. *kus* 'amplecti.'

No. 83b. W. *cwb* 'a concavity,' 'a kennel,' if a genuine word, seems = κύπη.

No. 84b. W. *cyn* 'wedge,' if not borrowed from *cuneus*, is cognate with that word and κῶνος.

No. 86. With the root LAK (whence λάκος, *lacer*) Nigra, *Rev. Celtique* i. 153, puts O.Ir. *du-rig* (gl. nudat) and other examples, to which add *dirgetar* (gl. exuantur) Ml. 136b., *du-n-dat-re-siu* (gl. quæ possit te ... exuere) Ml. 133a. *inderachtae l. huare narbu derachtae* (gl. successu prospero destitutum) Ml. 18d., *ro-deracht* (nudatum, exutum est) Corm. B. *s.v. Disert*. These Celtic words, like ῥάκος (Æol. βράκος), may all have lost *v* in anlaut.

No. 90. Ir. *mouichfid* 'magnificabit,' SM. iii. 30, (*oa = á*, Goidel². 55), Ir. *mocht* .i. *mór* 'magnus,' O'Cl., *mochtae* 'magnified,' 'glorified' = W. *maith* 'ample' (*cyn-faith, gor-faith, mawr-faith*) are cognate with the Lat. *macte* and the other words here noticed. And as metathesis of *r* is frequent, the Ir. *morc* (.i. *mór* 'magnus,' O'Cl.) may be = μακρό-ς.

No. 92. To the root MUK, whence μυκ-τήρ, *mungo*, etc., the Ir. *mucc* 'pig,' W. *moch* 'swine,' certainly belong.

No. 93. νέκυς. From a root ANK = NAK come Ir. *écaib, éc* 'death,' Corn., and Br. *ancou*, W. *angeu.*

No. 98. The Old-Welsh *pelechi* (gl. clavæ) Juv. 94, is either cognate with, or a loan from, πέλεκκος (*ch* ex *cc* as usual).

No. 99. πεύκη. O.Ir. *bi* (gl. pix), Z. 21, *bide* 'piceus,' Z. 792, W. *pyg*, Br. *pec*, are all loans. For the sinking of *p* to *b* cf. *brolach* = *prologus* and *lóc* (gl. osculum) Z. 28 = *pāc(em)*.

No. 100. Root τικ. O.Ir. *oech* 'enemy,' Corm., (with loss of initial *p*) is = A.S. *fâh*, Eng. *foe*, and (in form) Lith. *paika-s* 'unnütz, dumm' and is cognate with the OHG. *fêhjan* and other words here cited.

No. 102. Stem πλακ. Ir. *lecc* 'flagstone,' whence *lecán* (gl. lapillus) Z. 273, W. *llech* seems = *planca* : *liae*, gen. *liacc*, dat. *liicc*, a dissyllabic stem in *nc*, comes from a quite different root.

B

No. 106. The Irish *cerp* seems to belong to this Number. It is glossed by *teascad* 'a cutting,' O'Dav. 63, but rather means 'sharp :' *gorm-claidemh cerp cinntech or derg ima dorncur* 'a blue sharp sword, red gold (is) settled (to be) around its hilt,' and is = O.N. *skarp-r*, OHG. *skarph.*

No. 110. Stem σκαρπ. The W. *ysgarth* 'offscouring,' *ysgarthu* 'to purge out,' Ir. *ascartach* 'stuppa,' W. *carth*, belong either to this Number or to No. 53.

No. 111. Root SPAK, σκεπ. W. *paith* 'a glance,' 'a prospect,' 'a scene' (Spurrell) = Lat. *-spectus* in *conspectus, adspectus, prospectus*, should be added.

No. 112. Ir. *sciath* 'shield,' W. *ysgwyd*, O.Br. *scoet*, certainly go with σκιά, σκιάς. From the root SKA come not only Old-Irish *scáth, scáterc* 'mirror' = *scáth-derc*, but Corn. *scod*, Br. *squeut* 'ombre.' The Irish *cathair* a *c*-stem, W. *caer*, cannot be separated from *castrum* (ex *scad-trum*), the combination *str* losing *s* in Irish, *st* in Welsh, here as in Ir. *sethar-*, Z. 855, W. *chwaer* pl. *chwïor-ydd* = *svistr-*, Goth. *svistar* and in Ir. *fethal* (gl. ephoth) Tur. 87 = Skr. *vastra-m*, Gr. γίστρα (= Fεστρα) στολή, Hesych.

No. 113. To σκῦτος, κύτος, *cutis, húd* (root SKU 'to conceal'), the Welsh *cwd* m. 'cod,' 'pouch' in *ceill-gwd* 'scrotum,' and *ffar-god* [*ffar* ex *spar-*, Skr. *sphāra, sphira*, Lat. *spero* in *pro-spero*] 'a big paunch,' certainly belongs. The Ir. *ceo* 'mist' may also come from SKU. With σκεῦος, σκευάζω, (root SKYU, SKU, Fick, 209) I connect W. *ysgwd* 'a push,' 'a jet,' and perhaps Ir. *scoth* 'flower.'

No. 116. ἄγος. See at No. 120.

No. 117. To the root AG belong Ir. *ágh* .i. *cur* 'pone,' *ághaid* .i. *cuirid* 'ponunt,' O'Cl., the simplex of the forms cited by Windisch : *aige* .i. *graifne ech* 'horse-race,' Corm. Tr. 115, s.v. *mag, ágh* 'contest' (ἀγών, Lat. *ind-ágon-*) .i. *cath*, O'Cl., gen. *ága* (*déca a rigu rem n-aga*, Seirgl. Conc. : *indlema ind ága ernbais*, Rev. Celt. i. 37) : *ár*, W. *aer* (ex *agro*), 'battle,' 'slaughter,' and *ám* (gl. manus 'a body of persons'), Z. 268, a neuter stem in *men*, identical in every respect with *agmen*. In the British languages *g* disappears between vowels. We find accordingly W. *af*, *yd-a-f* 'ibo,' Z. 579, = Corn. *yth-af*, 580, Br. *a-ff*, 581, Cymr. *aet* ('eat'), Z. 585, = Lat. 3d sg. imper. *agito.*

No. 120. αἴξ. With Skr. *aja* 'buck,' ex *aga*, Rhys puts W. *ewig* 'doe' (ex *agikä*) ; as with ἄγος, No. 116, he puts the Welsh adj. *ew-og* 'guilty' (ex *agäka*). The Ir. *agh* f., which O'Clery explains by *bó* 'cow,' occurs in the Senchas Mór ii. 238, 254, meaning 'a bullock-calf,' and is probably cognate with *aja*. The acc. pl. *aige* (cf. *litre*, Z. 246) means 'deer' in the Táin bó Fráich : *dosennat na .uii. naige do ráith chruachan* 'they chase the seven deer to Rathcroghan.'

No. 121. Root *arg*. W. *ariant* = *argentum* should be quoted as preserving the *n*, which in Irish *arget* is lost before *t*.

No. 122. Ir. *guaire* .i. *uasal*, Corm. Tr., p. 91, is surely cognate with γαῦρος.

No. 123. γάλα. With the Skr. *jala-m* 'water' here cited cf. Ir. *gil* .i. *uisge* 'water,' O'Cl.

No. 128. The original *a* of the root GAN appears in W. *ganedig* 'natus' (*geni* 'nasci'), Br. *ganet* 'ortus' (*guenell* 'nasci'). To the Irish words here cited should be added *in-gen* 'filia,' *gean* .i. *bean* 'mulier,' O'Cl., *gean* .i. *inghean*, O'Cl., and *gnia* (= γνήσιος ?) .i. *mac seathar* 'filius sororis,' O'Cl., a later form of which, *niae*, Windisch wrongly puts at No. 342. It is to be wished that Windisch had given his opinion as to the relation (if any) between the words treated under this Number and the numerous Celtic derivatives from a root CAN :—the Gaulish *onos* 'filius'— the Irish *cana* 'cub,' W. *cenaw* (cf. Gaulish *Canaus*, *Canavilus* ?); *cenél* 'tribe'=W. *cenedl* f. γίνεθλον, γενέθλη, Ir. *cinis* 'orta est,' Brocc. h. 4, 3rd pl. *ro-chinset*, *rochinnset* [a], Z². 464, *ciniud iar tuistiu* 'bringing forth after begetting,' Senchas Mór i. 256.

No. 129. γέρανος. The Welsh *garan*, the Gaulish *tri-garanus,* should have been quoted in preference to the doubtful *grén* (ex *gresno*, root *gras* ?)

No. 133. γῆρυς. The Irish *gáir* 'cry' = W. *gawr*, should have been cited here. Also the O.Ir. *adgaur* [b] (gl. convenio ' I accost,' ' I suc '), Z. 428, whence *ad-ro-gar-t*, etc., Z. 455, *at-gairith*, Z. 994.

No. 133b. Ir. *glicc*, compar. *gliccu* 'sapientior,' Z. 276, *isin-glicci* ('in astutia'), Z. 248, seems cognate with Goth. *glaggvus* and Gr. γλαυκός. The primeval Celtic form may have been *gla-n-c-vo*, a becoming *i* as in *ingor* = *ancora*, Z. 5.

No. 135. Root γνω. Add *in-gnaidi* 'intellectus,' Ml. 63a, *in-gnae* 'intelligentia,' Ml. 44d, *co asa-gnoither nand sechmadachte* ('that it may be known that it is not a preterite '), Z. 743, *etar-gne* 'cognitio,' *etar-geuin* 'agnovit,' *itar-gninim* 'sapio prudentia.' The O.Ir. *gnáth* [c] ('solitus,' 'consuetus '), Z. 16, and W. *gnawd* are identical with γνωτός, (*g*)*notus*, and should be here cited, as preserving (like Lat. *gná-ru-s*) the original vowel. So Ir. *gnó* .i. *oirdeirc* 'conspicuus,' O'Cl., is = the Lat. *gnávu-s*, whence *gnávare*, *návare* 'to shew,' 'to exhibit.' In the following Irish words from O'Clery's Glossary the *g* is lost, *nós* 'custom,' *noudh cearda* .i. *oirdhearcaighim ealadha* [*noud* = Lat. *noto* : cf. *noadh* .i. *urdarcughadh*, *nuithear* .i. *oirdearcaigther*, O'Don. Supp.] *nois* .i. *oirdheirc*, *do-noisigh* 'notavit,' *noitheach* .i. *oirdheirc*. With the other Latin *gnávus* 'active,' the Irish *gnó* 'business,' *gnó(th)ach* 'busy,' are cognate. The O.Ir. *cia do-gnia* .i. *cia do aithéonta*, O'Cl., seems the 2d pers. sg. of a reduplicated future from the root *gná* ' to know.' Hence, too, the O.W. *am-gnau-bot* 'conscientia,' Z. 1056.

No. 140. ἐπείγω, ingāmi. The Old-Irish *ing* 'danger,' *as-cach-ing donforslaice taithmet anma Ignati* 'from every danger may the commemoration of Ignatius' name deliver us !' Goidel². 122, seems to belong to this Number. So also O'Reilly's *ing* 'force' (cf. *di-ing* 'impossibilis,' Z. 863), *ing* 'a stir,' if only these words are authentic. O'Clery glosses *ing* by *éigen* 'necessitas.'

No. 141. Root Ϝεργ, ἔργον. Not only O.W. *guery* (gl. efficax), but the Gaulish *vergo-bretus* and the O.Ir. *ferg* .i. *laech* 'hero,' Corm. Tr. 80, O'Dav. 84, should be added. So, too, *com-orgair* 'help,' O'R., if the word be genuine.

---

[a] Liquids in position are often doubled, Z. 41.
[b] Wrongly connected (Kuhn's Zeitschrift, xxi 430) with ἀγείρω. See Z. 1021, *ad-gaur* l. *duttluchur*.
[c] Hence *guás* 'consuetudo,' Z. 25.

No. 142. Root Γερχ, εἴργνυμι. O.Ir. *braig* 'chain,' SM. i. 6, *braga* (gen. *brayat*) 'prisoner,' Corm. Tr. 24, go with ἐ(Ϝ)έργω, etc. Here *br* is from *vr* as in *bran, briathar, bróen*, etc. And as *rg* often becomes *rc* (Z². 61), we may also compare the O.Ir. verb *do-farcai* 'cingit' in the St. Gall verses (Z². 953):—

Domfarcai fidbaidæ[a] *fál*
fomchain lóid luin luad nad cél
huas moldrán indlinech
fomchain trírech inna néu.

Me cingit dumeti sepes :
mihi sonat merulæ cantus celer quem
non celabo :
super meo libello interscripto
mihi sonat melodia avium.

Fommchain cói menn medair mass
himbrot glass de dindgnaib doss.
debrath nomchoimmdiu cóima
cáin scribaimm foroid [*n-óibda*].

Mihi sonat cuculi loquela clara,
pulcra,
in pallio glauco e summitatibus
arbustorum,
debrath (?) o meo domino epuli,
bene scribo ad symphoniam amœnam.

No. 146. The Ir. *lesc* (gl. piger) for *lecs (as *losc* for *locs = λοξός), n. pl. *leiscc*, Z. 67, Br. *lausq*, is identical in form and meaning with Lat. *laxus* and should be here cited. Why (may I venture to ask) does not Curtius connect with λήγω here noticed the O.Sax. *slac* 'hebes,' Eng. *slack*, OHG. *slah*? As Aufrecht points out (*Trans. Philolog. Soc.*, 1867, p. 20), the Homeric ἄλληκτος, ἀπο-λλῆξαι shew that λήγω has lost an initial consonant. So in the cognate Ir. *logmait* 'dimittimus,' *loghdha* .i. *lagsaine* 'slackness,' O'Cl., and in *lag*, O.Ir. *lac* ex *la-n-ga*, to be compared with *la-n-guidus*.

No. 150. Root μελγ. Add O.Ir. *tomlacht* (= *do-fo-mlacht*) .i. *bleghan no crudh* 'milk or curd,' O'Cl.

No. 152. The Ir. *ferg* 'anger' (= ὀργή) is from VARG. The Irish forms *broghadh* .i. *biseach* 'increase,' *broghdha* .i. *iomarcach*, *broghain* .i. *iomarcaigh no cccoir* 'excess,' O'Cl., *brogais* 'crevit,' O'Don. Supp., come from VRAG.

No. 153. ὀρέγω. In *Rigid a laim seacha cotuc meis combiud doib* 'he stretches his hand across her and brought them a dish with food,' Tochmarc Bec-fola, II. 2. 16, col. 767, the Irish cognate means 'porrigere.' Ir. *rogh* .i. *geis* 'prohibition,' O'Cl., and *recht = W. rhaith* belong to this Number.

No. 154. O.Ir. *lig* [leg. *líg*?] .i. *dath* 'colour :' *mesir liga asa saoire 7 asa suthaine* 'thou shalt estimate colours by their nobleness and by their lastingness,' O'Dav. 103, seems cognate with ῥηγεύς.

[a] See Nigra, *Reliquie Celticke* i. 23, and note that *fidbaidæ* is the gen. sg. of *fidbad* governed by the subsequent *fál* (Z. 915): that the verb *fo-chain* means 'sonat :' *im chloc focain cethra* ('for a bell which cattle sound'), Senchas Mór i. 126, 142 : that the adjective *luad* (better *lúath*) agrees with *lóid*, not with *luin*, the gen. sg. of *lou*: that *medair* is O'Clery's *meadhair* .i. *caint no urlabhra*, and means neither 'metri' (=Ir. *metir*, Z. 915) nor 'hilaris' (Rev. Celt. i. 479); that *brot* is the dat. sg. of *brat* 'pallium,' and does not mean 'cespite :' that *debrath* is explained (?) by *délabrath* (*Debrath ebraice brath* .i. *loquella debrath din délabrath*, II. 2. 16, col. 99): that *cóima* is the gen. sg. of *cóim* 'a feast,' O'Reilly's *caomh :* and that *coimmdiu cóima* is to be compared with *fiadu fírén na flede* 'deus justus dapis,' scil. eucharistiæ) Rumann in Laud 610, fo. 10. a. r. In the last line *oid* may possibly be the acc. sg. of *oid* (*oidh* .i. *ceol, odh* .i. *ceol*, O'Cl.) Fél. June 1. O'Curry's rendering of these verses, in his *Manners and Customs*, etc., ii. 387, is a curiosity.

No. 155. Root στεγ. The Old-Welsh *tig* (in *bou-tig* 'stabulum') now *ty* pl. *tai*, Corn. *ti*, later *chy*, Br. *ty* 'maison' shew that the root to which the Celtic words are referrible ends in *g*, not *c*. No. 156. Corn. *fràu* 'crow,' Br. *frau* 'choe,' 'monedula' point to a root SPRAG (= Skr. *sphurj*). Hence also W. *ffraeth* 'eloquent' ex *spracta, *sprag-ta*: cf. A.S. *sprëcan*, NHG. *sprechen*. Other instances of British *F* from *SP* will be found at Nos. 113, 157, 176b. 390, 652, and compare :—
W. *ffroen* 'nostril,' Ir. *srón* (gl. nasus), Z. 23, ex *sprogna*, with *spargere*;
W. *ffrwst* 'haste' ex *sprud-to*, with Goth. *sprauto* 'schnell;'
Corn. *felja* 'to split,' Br. *faut* 'fissura' ex *SPALT, with *spalten*.

No. 157. Br. *faez* 'vaincu' ex SPAC-TA, like Zend ςρας, seems cognate with σφίγγω, *spa-n-ge*, etc.

No. 158. With ὑγρός Siegfried equated the Ir. *úr* 'fresh,' 'new,' 'green' (*húrda* gl. viridarium, *hurdae* gl. viridia, *úrdatu* gl. virore, *n-uraigedar* gl. cui virere). Cf. W. *ir* 'juicy,' 'fresh,' 'green.' I doubt if *oss* (gen. *ois*, Senchas Mór i. 272) 'deer' (whence *oisín* 'fawn'), a masc. *a*-stem = Skr. *vastu* 'goat,' has anything to do with the Welsh *n*-stem *ych* 'bos' which Windisch places under this Number. The Irish *ess* 'ox' (Corm. s. v. *Essem*) is the cognate word, and both may be referred to the root VAGH, No. 169.

No. 159. With *vegeo, vigeo, vigil* put also the O. Ir. *diuchtrad* 'suscitatio,' Z 856, ex *di-og-t-rad, *di-fog-t-rad*.

No. 165. O. Ir. *arg* 'hero,' Corm. Tr. 2, O'Dav. 48 (gen. sg. *airg*, Corm. s. v. *Lorg*, dat. pl. *argaib*, Seirgl. Conc.) is certainly = ἀρχός : cf. also the following specimen of native etymology : *arg* [.i.] *fiann* 'champion' .i. *tiachar* ('it comes') ab Arg[iv]is .i. *o grecaib* ('from the Greeks') *ar febus an occ* 'because of their warriors' excellence,' O'Mulc. 57, H. 2, 16, col. 89.

No. 166. Root ἀχ, ἀγχ. Add *ochte* 'angustia,' Z. 68, *tachtæ* (*do-achtæ*) gl. augustus, Sg. 60b., *tachtad* (gl. aggens), Sg. 14b., *cumcigim* (*cum-ac-igim*), gl. ango, Z. 435. The Gaulish *octo-* in *Octodurus* 'arx in angustia sita,' Glück, KN. 133, is also probably cognate.

No. 166b. Ebel, Beitr. ii. 174, puts O. Ir. *bróen* 'pluvia,' Z. 31, with βρέχω, *rigo*, Goth. *rign*. Here, as in *bran* and *briathar*, *br* is from *vr*.

No. 167. To the root *dhragh* here postulated I refer the Irish nasalised forms *imm-drang* (O'Clery's *iomdhrang* .i. *comtharraing*) 'circumtrahere' and *tri-an-drong* .i. *tri deocha* 'tres haustus,' three *draughts*.

No. 168. Fick² 391 connects ἐλέγχω, ἔλεγχος, here cited, with Ir. *lingim* 'salio.' The Ir. *léim* 'saltus' ex *léngven*, O.W. *lammam* 'salio' ex *langvâmi*, are also cognate with Skr. *langh* 'to jump over,' 'to disregard,' 'to violate.'

No. 169. Glück (Neue Jahrbücher, 1864, p. 599) connects with *vah*, ὄχος, *veho* the Gaulish *co-vinnus* (ex *covignos*, as Ir. *cunn* ex *cug-no-s*) and the Welsh *cy-wain* 'vehere,' *ar-wain* 'ducere,' *am-wain* 'circumducere.' To this Number may also belong the Irish *ess* 'ox' = W. *ych* (pl. *ychen* = Corn. *ohan*) ex *vexan* (see *infra*, at No. 589), Goth. *auhsa* (as the beast of draught), and Lat. *uxor* (as she who is led home : cf. *uxorem ducere*).

No. 173. Root λεχ. Add O. Ir. *laige* 'concubitus' (*oc laige la mnái*, Corm. s. v. Orc tréith. In *con-lé* .i. *cob-lige* 'coitus,' Corm. Tr. 49, as in the causal *la-ai l* .i. *cuirid* 'ponunt,' O'Cl. (cf. Goth. *laqja*, τίθημι), *ro-la-sid* 'posuistis,' Z¹. 464, the *g* is lost between vowels (Z². 63, 1083). In *nach laighfedh* .i. *nach cuirfedh*, II. 3,18, p. 210, and in the expressions *laigid for* 'superiacet,' 'anteponitur,' *ni laig for* 'non superiacet,' O'Don. Supp. (cf. Goth. *liga*, κεῖμαι) the *g* is kept.

No. 174. Root λιχ. Add Ir. *ligur* 'tongue,' Corm., W. *llyaw* 'to lick,' Br. *leat.* So probably Ir. *liagh* 'ladle,' O'Don. Supp. (gen. sg. *na leighe*, acc. *leig*, Book of Aicill, 212) (= W. *llwy* 'spoon,' Br. *loa* 'cullier,' 'cochlear'), which is certainly cognate with the Latin *ligula*, *li-n-gula* 'spoon,' 'ladle,' 'skimmer.'

No. 176b. The W. *ffraw* (from SPRAG) 'state of motion,' *ffraw-dd*, 'stir,' etc., seem cognate with σπέρχομαι. For *ff* ex *sp* see No. 156.

No. 178. Root τρεχ. The Old-Celtic *ver-tragos* 'a swift dog' is quite authentic, and should have been here cited. See Glück, Neue Jahrbücher 1864, p. 597. So also W. *tro* = τρόχος (Br. *tro* 'tour'), O.W. *traet* 'pedes' = Ir. *traigid*, Br. *troat* 'pes.' The Irish *doich* .i. *luath* 'swift,' O'Cl., seems = ταχύς for τακυς, Skr. *taku* here cited. See above at No. 37.

No. 189. The Irish *gil* .i. *lám* 'hand' (O'Curry's transcript of the Brehon Laws, p. 1446) is identical with χείρ and the Old-Latin *hir* [a]. So *gillae* 'servus' is to be compared in root and meaning with χείριος, ὑπο-χείριος, in meaning with Lat. *man-cipium*. *Geilsine* .i. *munteras* 'famulatio,' LU., cited by O'Don. Supp., is also connected: the suffix *sine* also in *coceilsine* 'societas,' and *fáithsine* 'prophetia,' Z. 77. The Brehon-law *geil-fine*, the junior division of the Irish family, perhaps meant originally the father and those of his sons who were *in mancipio ejus.* The root is *ghar* 'rapere,' whence also Lat. *hirudo*, Ir. *gil* (Corm. Tr. 83), W. *gel*, Corn. *ghel* (gl. sanguissuga).

The resemblance of Ir. *cron* in *dio-chron* .i. *gan aimsir* 'without time,' O'Cl., to χρόνος here cited, is accidental. Fick 73 connects with χρόνος the O.N. *gran-n* 'gray.' This adjective seems identical with the Ir. *grant* .i. *liath.*

No. 193. The Celtic words for '*yesterday*' are possibly cognate with *heri* (*hesi*, *hjesi*), Ir. *(ind)hé*, Z. 609, W. *doe*, Corn. *doy*, Z. 617, 618 (ex *djai*, *jasi* ?), Br. *dech*, Z. 618, ex *djehi*, as *pelloch*, Z. 298, ex acc. sg. *perjóhen*, *perjósen.*

No. 197. Here Ir. *gel* 'white' is put with χλωρός, *haris*, *helvus*. I would rather connect it with χαλ-κός, No. 182. Curtius' theory, here stated, that the *f* in *flāvus* comes from *gh*, is rendered at least questionable by Irish *bla* (leg. *blá*) .i. *buidhe* 'yellow,' O'Dav. 56 and O'Cl., whence the dissyllabic man's-name *Bláán*, Fél. Aug. 10. See too Fick's Wörterbuch² 381. 'An. *blá-r*, Ahd. *blá* heisst auch *flavus* (nach Schade).'

No. 200b. The O.Ir. *gromma* 'satire,' *gromfa* 'he will satirize,' Corm. Tr. 86, *grim* .i. *cogadh*, O'Cl., *gruaim* 'morositas,' *gruamda* (gl. acer), Ir. Gl. 1065, W. *grwm* 'a murmur,' 'a growl,' all seem to belong to the root GHRAM, whence χρεμίζω, χρόμη, *fren-dere*, etc.

---

[a] Another O.Ir. word for 'hand' is *cor*, acc. sg. *coir* .i. *láim*, Fél. Dec. 12, (the Franciscan copy) in *ten-chor* (πυρολαβίς), Z. 81. Cf Skr. *kara*.

No. 201. O. Ir. *gert* [a] .i. *lacht* 'milk,' O'Dav. 94, was equated by Siegfried with Skr. *ghṛta* 'ghee;' and certainly belongs to the root GHAR 'to sprinkle.'

No. 204. Here, following Glück, KN. 24, the Gaulish particle *ande*, the Irish *ind*, *inn*, are equated with ἀντί, Skr. *anti*, Lat. *ante*, etc. But, first, the Irish form (we know nothing certain of the meaning of the Gaulish *ande*) not only implies motion to or against (*ind-rid* 'incursus,' *ind-eoin* 'anvil' = W. *ingion*, Br. *anneffn*, all ex *ande-vani), but also motion from something (cf. *ind-arpae* 'ablatio'), and, secondly, the tenuis in the combination NT is always (so far as I know) preserved in Gaulish [b]. In Irish (except in loan-words like *cland* = planta, *talland* = talentum) the dental is kept, while the nasal disappears, often lengthening the preceding vowel, as in *cét*, *tét*, *dét* = W. *cant*, *tant*, *dant*. We should accordingly expect the Irish cognate of ἀντί, etc., to begin with *ét-*, and this actually occurs in *étan* 'forehead' (dat. sg. *étun*: *atracht in lúan láith asa-étun* 'the hero's light [e] rose out of his forehead,' Táin bó Cúalnge), which I unhesitatingly put with the Latin *antiæ* 'forelock,' and the OHG. *endi* 'forehead,' Fick 425. The British cognate of ἀντί is (as might be expected) the Br. *ent*, Z. 616. The Latin cognate to *ande-*, *ind-*, *inn-* seems *ind-* in *ind-igeo*, *ind-ustria*, *ind-ulgeo*, *ind-ūgo*, *ind-uo*.

No. 206. For *i-fhus*, *i-fhos* read *i-fus*, *i-fos*. Windisch should have noted here that in the *Lebar Brecc* and in Codex A of Cormac's Glossary (from which he cites these forms) the dotted *f* is used not only to express the *f* infected by flanking vowels, but also the *f* changed to *v* by the influence of a preceding nasal. Ir. *tas* .i. *comhnaidhe* 'a dwelling,' O'Cl. may be = *do-vastu*.

No. 208. *Saith* (.i. *ionnmhas* 'treasure,' O'Cl.) ex *sati and the synonymous *sét* ex *sant-o are cognate with ἐτεός, *satya*, *sóth*. The Gaulish name name *Santones*, is also referrible to this Number.

No. 209. O.W. *at-*, *et-*, Z. 900, Corn. *as-*, Br. *az-*, *at-* should be added to ἔτι, &c.

No. 211. Ϝιταλός. With *vatsa* Siegfried equated the Mediæval Latin (Gaulish?) *vassus*, W. *gwas*: cf. O.Ir. *ainder* (W. *anner*) 'heifer,' 'young woman.'

No. 214. πέτομαι. O.Ir. *étar* 'impetratur,' Z. 504, should have been placed with Goth. *fintha*. The Old-Welsh *ataned* [d] 'wings,' *atanocion* (gl. alligeris) Rev. Celt. i. 360 (cf. Ir. *ethaite*, O'Don. Supp.) preserves the *a*-vowel. So the O.Ir. *aith* (gl. pinna) = **pāti-*, *deáith* (gl. bipennis), which Zeuss, Gr. C. 301, wrongly puts among the examples of the diphthong *ái*. They should be transferred to p. 17.

No. 216. Root στα. The British cognates of ἵ-στημι, *sto*, etc., come from an extended root STA-M, losing the *t* as usual: W. *sefyll*, *safiad*, etc.,

---

[a] *Cen gert ferbba* (sine lacte vaccarum) LU. cited in Corm. Tr. 37.
[b] Cf. *argento-*, *carpento-*, *Nantuates*, *Commontorios*, etc. *Candetum* for *canteton, if genuine, is an exception.
[e] I venture to connect *lúan* (from **lucno-*) with Lat. *lúna*, *lúmen* (for *lucna, *lucmen) and Gr. λύχνος from λυχνος.
[d] 'Illa recondit (.i. *renovat*) opus (.i. *hí halaned*),' gloss recently found by Mr. Bradshaw in the Oxford copy of Ovid's *Ars Amatoria*.

Br. *seuell* 'surgere.' The W. *ystof*, Br. *steuffinn* arc loans from *stämen*. To the Irish words here cited add O'Clery's *seise* .i. *sesamh*. In his *stá* .i. *seas* (= siste)—'*stá a athaigh ar Conall*'—the *t* is kept.

No. 221. With στερίω cf. *serbh* 'theft' (O.Celtic *stervā), *fo-serba bega* .i. *mingata* 'petty thefts,' O'Dav. 117 : *searbhaidh* .i. *goid* 'theft,' O'Cl., *siorbhai* .i. *gadaigheacht* 'thieving,' O'Cl.

No. 222. στερεός. With this arc connected not only Ir. *seirt* .i. *neart* 'strength,' O'Cl., *ro-n-sert*, Fél. Ep. 11, *seiric* .i. *laidir* 'strong,' O'Cl., but also O.Ir. *us-sarb* 'death,' Corm. : 'gewiss,' says Curtius, 'heisst sterben eigentlich erstarren .... Die Begriffe starr, fest, stark berühren sich hier vielfach.'

No. 227. Add to the derivatives from the root STAR the O.Ir. *có-sair* .i. *leabaidh* 'lectus,' O'Cl., *sreith* (gl. strues) Z. 992, (gl. pratum) Sg. 20, W. *sarn* 'causeway,' *sarnu* 'to strew' and O.Ir. *fo-sernair* 'is spread abroad' (*foser-nair senfocal* 'vulgatur proverbium,' O'Dav. 54. To the by-form STRU (whence Goth. *strauja*) we may refer W. *y-strewi, trewi* 'sternutare,' Br. *struyaff*, and Ir. *sreod* 'sneezing,' 'the omen drawn from sneezing.'

No. 230. Three important Celtic derivatives from the roots TAN, TAM-P should be added—O.Ir. *tana* (*is-gann membrumm, is-tanu an-dub* 'parchment is scanty : thin is the ink,' Z. præf. xii) = W. *teneu*, Br. *tanau* : O.Ir. *tonach* .i. *léine* 'indusium' .i. *brat* 'pallium,' O'Cl. [a] ; and, lastly, O.Ir. *timpán* 'a small stringed instrument (Corm. Tr. 163, *tet* .i. *tiompán*, O'Cl.) played with a bow' (O'Curry, *Manners and Customs* iii. 362), which has nothing to do with *tympănum* [b], but is connected with the Lithuanian *timpa* 'sinew,' the O.N. *thömb* 'bowstring,' and perhaps also with the Latin *tempus*, *templum* and *temptare*. The Ir. *tan* 'time,' *in-tain* 'when,' Z. 708, also belong to this Number.

No. 231. *Tám* .i. *bas* O'Dav. 121 (*tám roselaig dúini* 'pestilentia quæ occĭdit homines,' Corm. 45), *tamh* .i. *plaigh*, O'Cl. and its derivative *taimthiu*, Fél. July 2, etc., seem, like *tābes*, to come from the root TAK.

No. 234. The Ir. *tummud* 'a dipping' (n. pl. tri *tuimthea* gléso in letraim dídenach, Lib. Arm. 78 a. 2), *tumud na cainnell*, Senchas Mór ii. 252, is for *tumbuth, *tungvătu, Lat. *tinguere*, just as the neuter *n*-stem *imm*, *imb* 'butter' is = Lat. *unguen*. In the root-vowel the Irish form agrees with OHG. *thuncon, duncon*. Other instances of hard *m* (*mb*) from *ngv* are :—

Ir. *remmad* 'to distort,' Corm. s. v. *reimm*, = *(*v*)*rengvătu*, ῥέμβειν, A.S. *vringan*, O.N. *rangr* ;

Ir. *léimm* 'leap,' Z. 1053, ex *lēngven (*langh* 'salire') ;

Ir. *cruim* .i. *toirneach* 'thunder,' O'Cl., ex *crongvi, O.N. *hrang* ; and

Ir. *dram* .i. *iomad* 'multitude,' O'Cl., ex *dra-n-gva : cf. *dru-n-gus* 'a force,' Ir. *drong*, O.Lat. *forc-tus*.

No. 235. The Ir. *tuag* 'bow,' Z. 22, and *tál* 'adze,' Ir. Gl. No. 252, Goidel. 59, like *τόξον*, and the Slav. *tesla* 'axe,' belong to this Number.

---

[a] *Tuinech* .i. *cochall*, O'Dav. 120, is a loan from *tunica*.
[b] Hence is borrowed Ir. *timpan* (with a short *a*), gen. sg. *timpain* : 7 *si oc senmaimm thimpain* 7 *oc cautain chiúil* 'and she, Miriam, sounding a timbrel and singing music,' LB. 118b, referring to Exodus xv. 20.

No. 236. W. *tlawd* 'poor,' 'needy' is = τλητός : cf. Ir. *tlaith ;* and with τέλος, meaning 'tax,' 'duty,' 'toll,' the Ir. *taile* (gl. salarium), Ir. Gl. No. 739, *tuarastal* (= *do-fo-ar-as-tala*) 'hire,' 'wages,' and W. *tal* 'payment' are certainly cognate. With Lat. *tollo* I would put Ir. *tall* .i. *goid* 'theft,' O'Cl., *tallsad* .i. *dogoidsead* 'they stole,' *ib.*, *teallsadar* (.i. *dogoidsead*, ib.) = O.Ir. *tellsatar*. In the *c*-stem *teol* 'thief,' O'Cl., [n. pl. *(bain)teolaigh* 'she-thieves'] an Old-Celtic *teulax*, we have the enhancement found in Skr. *tōlayāmi*. The Ir. *tlás* or *tlus* .i. *áirnéis no spréidh* (= præda) 'cattle,' O'Cl., and *tletid* 'tollunt,' O'Don. Supp., should also be added.

No. 237. The Irish *tét* .i. *sligi* 'road' from *tem-ta*, Goidel². 171, may belong to the root τεμ. So *sét* (O'Clery's *séd* .i. *samhail*) 'likeness,' Fél. June 16, is from *sim-ta :* cf. Lat. *simitu*, *simul*.

No. 239. Root τερ. The O.W. *tarater*, Corn. *tardar*, Br. *tarazr* 'terebrum' should be added.

No. 241. In the Irish *tair*, *terad* 'dry weather' [*ba-tair* (.i. *ba-terad*) *coidchi innagort* 'there was dry weather till night in her field,' Brocc. h. 30] no trace of the *s* of TARS is discoverable ; this *s* may therefore be regarded as a determinative, Fick 1013.

No. 242. The Old-Ir. *tethra* agrees in declension with τέτραξ. Its gen. sg. *tethrach* is glossed by *badb* 'scallcrow' in LU. 50a, top margin—Mac Lonan *dixit :*—

Mian mná tethrach [a] *atenid* [b]	'The she-scallcrow's longing is her fires [b],
slaide sethnach [c] *iarsodain*	Slashing of sides thereafter,
suba [d] *luba* [e] *folubaib* [f]	Blood, body under bodies,
ugail [g] *tróga* [h] *dir drogain* [i]	Eyes, heads (?), awful mutterings !'

So O'Clery : *teathra* .i. *badhb no feanog*.

No. 243. W. *tat* now *tâd*, Corn. *tâs*, Br. *tat* 'pater' are identical with *tata*, τέττα. Such words are unlikely to have been borrowed.

No. 247. Add O.Ir. *túithlae* (= *tū-tal-ia*), gl. gibbus, Z. 767 : *táare* 'cibus,' Z. 247, may also come from the root TU.

No. 251. Ir. *dub* 'dark' is cognate with Goth. *daubs* = 'deaf' and *du-m-b-s* = 'dumb,' and τυφλός if this be for *θυφλός.

No. 252. The Gaulish SVADV-RIX on the Besançon bronze knife (Rev. Celt. ii. 112) and the Irish name *Sadb* i. e. *Sadv*, all probably go with *sua(d)vis*, ἡδύς, *svādu*.

No. 258. Root δυϝ. Corn. *dewi, dewy* 'to blaze,' Br. *devi* 'brûler' belong to this.

No. 259. With δαί-ϛαλ-ο-ς, etc. the Br. *daladur* 'dolabra,' 'ascia,' 'dolabrum' seems cognate.

No. 260. O.W. *or dometic* (gl. domito), Z. 1057, *ardomaul* 'docilis,' Mart. Cap. 9. a. b., *ni cein-guo-demisauch* (gl. non bene passa, estis), Z. 1057, Br. *dauat* 'brebis,' might be here added to the derivatives from the root DAM.

---

[a] .i. *badb* 'scallcrow,' (*Rev. Celt.* i. 33), the *corvus cornix* or hooded crow.
[b] .i. *gle* 7 *arm* 'battle and arms.'
[c] .i. *tácb* 'side.'
[d] .i. *fuil* 'blood.'
[e] .i. *corp* 'body' (so O'Clery, *lubha* .i. *corp*).
[f] .i. *fo feraib* 'under men.'
[g] .i. *súli* 'eyes.'
[h] .i. *cend* 'head.'
[i] .i. *fúach* 'word.'

c

No. 261. Ir. *daif* 'a drink,' Corm. Tr. 61, reminds one of δέπας οἴνου 'eigentlich ein *Maass* Wein, von wo die Uebertragung auf das Gefäss leicht ist,' Curtius No. 261. The desiderative (?) formations Ir. *dibhe* .i. *tart* ' thirst,' O'Cl., and Gr. δίψα (ex ἱπ-σα) possibly meant originally ' a desire for a measure of liquor.'

No. 262. Ir. *dair* 'inire vaccam vel ovem,' gen. *dara*, Senchas Mór i. 144, ii. 45, *darmna*, Book of Aicill 230, O'Dav. 79, *con-da-ro-dar-t* ' eam, scilicet vaccam, inivit,' Rev. Celt. i. 44, seem cognate with ἑαρθάνω and *dor-m-io* : cf. the use of the Germ. *be-schlafen*.

No. 264. Root ἱε. To this or No. 260 belong O.Ir. *tuidme* (do-fo-DAM-ia or do-fo-DE-mia) ' colligatio,' ' conjunctio,' Fél. Oc. 17, Ep. 355, *oc-tuidme* Corm. s. v. Essem, *tuidmide* (gl. fixum), Z. 984.

No. 265. Root ἱεμ. Ir. *daimh* .i. *teagh* 'domus,' O'Cl., should be added.

No. 266. ἱεξιός. In W. *dcheu* ' right,' ' south,' Br. *deho*, the suffix resembles that of Goth. *taihs-va*.

No. 267. Root ἱερ. Br. *darn* ' pars,' W. *darn* ' a piece or patch ' (whence the English verb *to darn*) should be added.

No. 269. The instructive Old-Welsh *duiutit* (-*tit*= Lat. -*tūtem*) ' divinitas ' should have been cited, as well as the O.Ir. *doi* (*doi-duine* .i. *dag-duine*, Corm.) = *divus*, δῖος, and *tré-denus* ' triduum,' Z. 302.

No. 270. Root ἱο. Add *dan airgid* .i. *maoin no aisgidh airgid*, O'Cl., *dathadh* .i. *tiodhlacadh* ' a giving,' *ib*.

No. 279. Root ἱδ. Ir. *ithim* ' mando,' Z. 429, here cited, seems rather connected with *ith*, W. *yd* ' corn,' an *u*-stem = *pitu*. But O.W. *esicc* in *leu-esicc* (gl. cariantem), Beitr. vii. 388, now *ysig* ' corroding' is almost certainly from *ed-ticio*·

No. 280. Root ἱδ. The O.Ir. *sadb*, Corm., W. *haddcf* ' a dwelling' certainly (like Skr. *sadman*) belongs to this Number, though the suffix is obscure. So *aitheallach* (ex *aith-sedlach* ?) .i. *aith-suidhiughadh*, O'Cl. In *consádu* ' I set together,' Fél. Jan. 23, *adsuidet*, *arsaid*, SM. iii. 10, we have a causal meaning. In *adh* .i. *dligheadh* ' ge-setz,' O'Cl., (whence *adha*, *com-adas*, etc.) the initial *s* seems lost, as in *amal* ' instar' and the negative prefix *an*- = *sēmi*.

No. 284. Fick 30 refers κέκαδον, κεκαδόμην, with Lat. *cado*, *cēdo*, to a root *kad* 'gehen,' ' weichen,' ' fallen.' To this I would refer W. *cwyddo* ' to fall,' in *dy-gwyddo*, *tram-gwyddo*, *cwyddol* ' falling,' and Ir. *casair* .i. *cioth* ' a rainfall,' ' a shower,' O'Cl., ex *cad-tric*.

No. 286. Root μεδ. W. *meddwl* ' thought,' ' mind' belongs to this Number. Very beautiful is Windisch's explanation of *coimdiu* ' dominus ' as *con-midiu*. Compare *dia már midedar cach ní* (' a great God, who judges everything') Siaburcharpat Conculainn, LU., and the Old-Norse name for ' gods,' *rögn*, as μέδοντες.

No. 288. Root ὑδ. Corn. *eth* : *mar whek aga eth* ' so sweet their odour,' O. 1994. Here infected *d* in auslaut is regularly sharpened into *th*.

No. 291. Ir. *od* in *od-brann* (gl. talus = a Skr. *pada-bradhna* [a]), whence *uide* ' iter ' (= Vedic *padyā* ' fusstritt,' Grassmann), may (as Siegfried thought) have lost initial *p* and be connected with πούς, etc.

[a] Cf. *çata-bradhna* ' hundred-pointed.'

No. 298. With á(ϝ)ωεη (root VID) the Irish *faed*[a] 'cry,' W. *gwaedd* are identical. From the root VAD I would derive the Ir. *fuidhir* .i. *briathar* 'word,' O'Cl., and also the Irish *fonn* (from *fo-n-d*) 'a tune,' 'a song,' the root being nasalised as in Skr. *va-n-dê* 'celebro :' O.Ir. *ús* (ex *ud-tu*, *vad-tu*) .i. *slonnadh no aisneis*, O'Cl., *im-thús* (= *imm-do-ús*) 'history,' *imthúsa* 'tidings;' and *fasc* (ex *vadco*) 'nuntiatio' SM. i. 258.

No. 300. ὕδ-ωρ. Add *os* (= *ud-ta*) in *os-bretha* 'water-judgments,' SM. i. 182. The nasalised form *fa-n-d* ('ainm na dére') occurs in LU. 45a with the meaning 'tear.' It also seems to occur in *di-unnach* 'capitolavium,' Corm., *diunnach* .i. *glanadh o pheacadh* 'cleansing from sin,' O'Cl., and in *foinsi* .i. *tiobrada no toibre* 'wells,' O'Cl.

No. 302. Stem αἰϑ. W. *aidd* 'calor,' 'studium,' Br. *oaz* should be added. The O.Ir. *ésce*, *ésca* 'moon,' Z. 229, (ex *êd-cio*, as *usce* 'water' ex *ud-cio*) seems, like Lat. *eidus*, *idus*, Skr. *i-n-du*, referrible to a root ID.

No. 303. Root ἀλϑ. To this Number surely belong Lat. *arduus*, Gaulish *ardvo* (in *Ardu-enna*), Ir. *ard*.

No. 306. Root ἐρυϑ. W. *rhudd* 'ruddy,' Br. *ruz*, should be added.

No. 307. Root ϑα, ϑη. Add M.Br. *di-zonaff* 'ablactare.'

No. 309. Root ϑε. Add O.Ir. *in-denim* (gl. debilitatum), Parker 115, pl. *indenmi* (gl. imbecilles), Z. 860.

No. 312. Fick 99 puts the Gaulish *dunum* (*dûnon*) with *dhanu*, θίς.

No. 313. With θίω, θοός, has been compared the Ir. *dó* in the common phrases *dó duit dotig* 'go thou[b] to thy house,' LU. 45b. ; *do duit uaim* 'go thou from me,' *ib.* 47a; *dó dúib iarom dia-saichthin* 'go you then to her,' *ib.* 110a. But, like *dothar* .i. *abann* 'river,' *duithir na hoidche* .i. *maidin* 'morning,' O'Cl., it rather seems cognate with δύω, δύνω, OIIG. *zûwen*, Fick². 95.

The verb θήγω 'I sharpen' here mentioned is compared by Fick 772 with O.N. *dengja*, A.S. *dencgan* 'to hammer.' Whether he is right or wrong, these Teutonic verbs seem cognate with the Irish *dedaig* 'compressit' Goidel². 133, *lase for-ru-dedgatar* (gl. obprimendo), Ml. 63a, *for-dengat* (gl. opprimentes), Ml. 29a, *for-dingit* 'opprimunt,' LB. 39a, *for-dengar* (gl. deprimitur), Ml. 57d, *for-diastar* 'opprimetur,' O'Dav. 77, 85, *for-n-diassatar* (gl. opprimi), Ml. 39b.

No. 315. Glück (Neue Jahrb. 1864, p. 600) connects Ἀνδράστη, the name of a British goddess of victory, with Skr. *drsh* 'vincere,' and translates 'die unüberwindliche.' The Ir. substantive *dorr*, gen. *dorre* (= θάρσος?) explained by *fearg* 'ira,' O'Cl., and the adjective *dorr* .i. *aggarb no royharbh* 'harsh or very rough,' O'Cl., may also belong to this Number.

No. 317. Root ϑρε. To this, I think, belong two Celtic words: Ir. *drogain*, which is glossed by *fúach* supra No. 242, and *dord* 'susurrus,' Corm. s. v. adann = W. *dwrdd*, whence O.Ir. *dordaid dam* 'mugit cervus,' LU., *fo-dordchu* (gl. susurratores), Z. 72. With *drog(ain)* cf. (τον)θορυγέω. In the neut. *n*-stem *deil-m* 'sound,' 'thunder,' the *r* has become *l*.

---

[a] Dat. sg. *faeid*, Corm. s. v. bachall.   [b] Lit. 'a going to thee.'

No. 319. Ούρα. The Gaulish *dvorico* should be cited as showing the Old-Celtic anlaut which agrees with that of *dvāra*.

No. 320. Root Ϩυ. To this belongs Ir. *duine* 'homo,' W. *dyn*, as the 'thinker' (cf. Lith. *dù-ma-s* 'gedanke') : the diphthongal plural of *duine* (*dóini*) either shows an abnormal enhancement of the root-vowel or belongs to No. 308.

No. 324. Ir. *fe-n-did*, *fennid* 'champion' seems from the root *radh*. So perhaps the *s*-future *fess* .i. *muirfidh* 'occidet,' O'Cl.

No. 325. Neither Ir. *uth* 'mammula' (cf. Lat. *uter*?) nor W. *uwd* 'pap' can possibly be cognate with οὖθαρ. An Irish dat. pl. *indib* translated 'udders' in a gloss on the Book of Aicill, p. 228, is perhaps the Celtic relative required. The O.Ir. *indeb* 'profit,' Z². 789 (= *inncamh* .i. *biseach* increase,' O'Cl.) may be in root = Lat. *über* 'fullness,' 'richness,' 'fertility' ex *vanfer*, *vanθer*.

No. 326. For the words which Windisch here erroneously refers to the root BHADH, we may substitute the following :—from the unnasalised form, we have Ir. *buiden*, O.W. *bodin* pl. *bodiniou* (gl. phalanges), *byddin* 'a band,' 'a troop,' O.Ir. *basc* 'monile' (= *bad-co*), Corm. 7, with which W. *baich* 'a burden,' 'bundle,' Br. *bech* = Lat. *fascis* (ex *bhadci-s*) may, I think, be connected ; from the nasalised form we have Ir. *band* .i. *dliged* 'lex,' in the Vocabulary in the Lebar Lecain (= O'Clery's *bann* .i. *dligheadh*) [a] *for-bann* 'bad or false law,' O'Don. Supp., *co-forbannach* 'κακονομιστί' (if one may coin a Greek word), LB. 60b, and the adjective *bind* 'melodious,' *bindiu* (gl. sonorius), Z. 275, which is to be compared with Lat. *fides* 'the string of a musical instrument,' and the nasalised forms *of-fend-ix*, *of-fend-imentum*.

No. 338. The W. *sarff* is identified by Ebel (Beitr. ii. 158) with Skr. *sarpa* : but it is probably a loan (like Br. *sarpant*) from *serp*(*ens*).

No. 341. Cormac's *rop* 'animal rumpens' (gen. *ruip*, acc. pl. *rupu*) may belong to this Number : his *rap* 'animal rapiens' to No. 331 (cf. Ital. *rappare*). From *rop* we have the abstract *roptene* .i. *gairge* in H. 3, 18, p. 73, col. 3.

No. 343. The Ir. *aicc* 'bond,' O'Don. Supp., *aigter* (leg. *aicther*) 'is tied,' 'is fastened,' ib., *aice* .i. *trebhaire* 'a surety' (vas, vadis) ib., *aicde* .i. *cumtach* 'a structure,' Corm., *aicde airgit* .i. *dealg no fail* 'a pin' [cf. πάσσαλος, *palus*] or 'ring,' O'Don. Supp., *aicce ab accula* (leg. *acula* 'a little needle') II. 2. 16, col. 88, all appear to have lost initial *p* and to come from a nasalised form (cf. *pa-n-go*) of the root PAG. What are *ágai umaidi*, LU. 24b?

No. 345. Παλάμη and *palma* are represented not only by the Irish *lám* (= *plāma*), but by the adjective *dilmain* 'liber' (= *di-plămani*, lit. 'e-man-cipatus'), compar. *dilmainiu* (gl. liberius), Ml. The noun *palf*, which occurs in Welsh, Cornish and Breton, is no doubt a loan from *palma*.

No. 350. The *p* of πατέομαι, *pasco*, etc., is preserved in the Old-Irish compound *úr-phaisiu* (gl. cancer, morbus), Z. 268, where *paisiu* is identical

---

[a] So Corssen refers Lat. *lex* (Osc. abl. sg. *ligud*) to the root LIG 'im sinne der bindenden satzung.'

with (perhaps borrowed from) *pastio*, and *úr* (.i. *olc*, Cormac) is cognate with *πύθω*, *pūs*, etc. No. 383.

No. 351. Stem *παυ*. Add W. *poues* (gl. quies), Z. 1053, and the Cornish *s-pauen mor* (gl. equor), where the *s* is prosthetic, as in Corn. *s-quenip* (Fr. 'guenipe'), Bret. *s-clacc* (Fr. 'glace'), *s-claer* (Fr. 'clair'), Irish *s-túag*, *τόξον*, *s-cipar* from Lat. *piper*, and *s-préidh* 'cattle' from Lat. *præda*.

No. 352. Ir. *li* 'color,' (gl. gloriam), Z. 623, W. *lliw* m., Br. *liu*, and the Ir. *alad* 'speckled' = Skr. *palita*, *πελιτνός*, may have all lost initial *p* and belong to *livor*, cited under this Number.

No. 353. *πέλλα* (ex *πελνα*). Cf. Ir. *lenn* (gl. sagana *vel* saga), Z. 1063, O.W. *lenn*, ib., ex *plenja*, Lith. *plëne* 'haut' Fick, Spracheinheit 338.

No. 355. In O.Ir. *putte* 'cunnus,' Corm. Tr. 138, compared with *πόσθη*, and Lith. *pyzdū* we have possibly an example of the assimilation of *s* to *t*, (here from *d* provected by *s*) which we certainly find in *nett* (W. *nyth*) = Lat. *nidus* ex *nisdus*. The following apparent examples of this assimilation are given merely as conjectures for the criticism of competent philologists :—

att 'tumor,' Fél. Prol. 18, Z. 949 ; cf. *ὄζος* (ex *ὀσδος*, Goth. *ast-s*), properly the *nodus* from which a branch springs ;

bet 'culpa,' Corm. Tr. 20, ex *besdo-* [*βέεσ-μα*, *βόó(σ)λος*] as the nearly synonymous *púdar* 'harm,' 'error' from Lat. *putor* ;

brót 'stimulus,' n. pl. *bruit*, LU. 93 = urdeutsch *brosda*, Fick 822 ;

ét 'zelus,' Z. 18 : cf. O.N. *œsta* 'etwas verlangen,' Fick 688 ;

etiuth (leg. *étiuth*) = *vestitus*, Z. 802, *étach* 'vestis,' Z. 810 ;

éitset 'auscultent,' *éit-s-ech-t* 'auditus,' Z. 996 : cf. O.Lat. *oisdier*, αἰσθ-ἐσθαι, Fick 429 ;

gataim 'rapio' : cf. Skr. *hasta* 'hand ;'

rét 'res,' Z. 18, ex *ré-s-tu* (as *áis* ex *aiv-as-tu*?).

No. 357. The W. *pell* 'far' (*pellach* 'ulterior'), Br. *pell* 'procul' certainly belongs to this Number. As to the liquids, O.Ir. *ire*, Z. 277, is = *περαῖος* = *pell*, just as O.Ir. *ferr* = *variyas* = *guell*. This and other instances at Nos. 341, 351, 358, 366 shew how groundless is Windisch's assertion (Vorrede, x) that 'indogerm. *p* im Keltischen *nie* erhalten ist.'

No. 358. *περάω*. W. and Br. *go-br* 'præmium,' W. *go-brwy* 'reward' (Old-Welsh *guo-pr*, *guo-prui*), *gobryn* 'merit,' *gobru* 'to compensate,' M.Br. *gopr merdeat* 'loyer de marinyer,' *gopra* 'loyer' all belong to this Number. The Gaulish *rito-n*, O.W. *rit* now *rhyd* 'a ford' may also belong to it, if we assume the loss of *p*.

No. 359b. Ir. *earc* .i. *breac* 'speckled,' O'Cl., is identical with *πέρκος*.

No. 360. *πέρυσι*. The form *in-uraid* (with one *n*), here cited from the Táin bó Fráich, is incorrect. It is an accusative of time, and should be *inn-uraid* or better (as in O'Mulconry's Glossary, No. 748, H. 2. 16, col. 117), *inn-uraith*. The Celtic representative of the Gothic *fairni-s* 'old' here cited seems the Old-Ir. *iarn* in Cormac's *iarn-bélre* or *iarm-bélre* 'an obsolete word' (see s.vv. *cloch, fern*). Here, as in the next words, we have loss of initial *p*[a].

---

[a] So Ir. *ossar* is = Lat. *posterus*, and cognate with *πύματος*, etc., Curtius, p. 706.

No. 363. Root πι. Add O.Ir. *ith* 'fat,' O'Don. Supp. and Cormac s.v. *itharnae* 'a rush-light' (*filum scirpeum*): Corn. *itheu* (leg. *iteu*) gl. ticio, Br. *eteó* 'brandon.'

No. 366. Root πλα. Add Irish *com-all* 'pregnant,' acc. sg. f. *comaill*, Brocc. h. 39 : *comhaille* .i. *at bronn* 'pregnancy,' lit. 'tumor ventris,' O'Cl. The form *rochomall* here cited by Windisch means *implevit* not *implevi*. The W. *lwydd* (ex *luid*, *léd*) in *arg-lwydd* may be = πληθύς or πλῆθος. The original *p* is retained in Gaelic *pailt* 'plenteous,' Corn. *pals (golcow pals leas myll*, P. 165, 3) and Br. *paot* • 'beaucoup,' 'plusieurs.'

No. 367. *Liach* may perhaps be connected with the root πλακ plan-g-o, etc. It occurs in Z. 624, *ba uisse hirnaigde erru ba liach anepeltu* 'it was right to pray for them : their perishing was lamentable.' So O'Clery (in that excellent glossary which it is a shame not to reprint), *Líach* .i. *ni as doilidh no as olc le duine.* unde *fiacha fer dá liach oir ba doilidh dó a athair do mharbhadh a ccath 7 a mathair d'ég aga bhreith* "what is grievous or evil to a human being : unde 'Fiacha, the man of two *liachs;*' for it was grievous to him that his father was slain in battle and that his mother died in bringing him forth."

No. 371. Root πο, πι, πω. W. *yfed*, Br. *evaff* 'boiro' should be put with Ir. (*p)ibimm* = 'bibo,' and W. *di-od*, Br. *di-et* 'boyre,' with Lat. *potare.* The Ir. *at* .i. *laith* 'milk,' O'Cl., *án* 'a drinking-cup,' Corn., and *ól* (*an ól meda* 'the drink of mead,' Brocc. h. 85) whence *ró-ólach* (gl. crapulatus vino), Goidel², 59, have all probably lost initial *p* and are connected with this root.

No 378. Root πρα. Add Ir. *láth* 'heat of animals in the season of copulation,' O'Don. Supp. The Ir. *luaith* 'ashes,' W. *lludw* come from a root (cf. Skr. *pru-sh*, *plu-sh* 'to burn') whose vowel is *u*.

No. 382. With Goth. *speiva* 'spuo' cf. W. *ffi.* The Br. *piffit* is borrowed from *pituita.*

No. 385. πῦρ. Add Ir. *úr* .i. *teine* 'ignis,' O'Clery.

No. 386. Fick's suggestion (*Spracheinheit* 341) that πυρός may be "das 'reine' Getreide"—cf. Lat. *purus*—derives support from the Irish *cruithnecht*, Corn. Tr. 33, which seems cognate with Lat. *scrutinium.*

No. 387. πῶ-λος. The O.Ir. dissyllable *haue* 'nepos,' Z. 229, (ex *páusio*?) seems to belong to this : cf. Lat. *pūsion-*, *pusiola.* But *óa* 'minor,' = W. *iau*, Skr. *yaviyas*, and *oam* (leg. *óam*) 'minimus' have lost initial *y*.

No. 389. Root σπαρ. To this Number belong Ir. *spréd* 'a spark,' Corn. tenlam : *spreite arfed senlebor* 'scattered throughout old books,' W. *ffrid*, *ffrit* 'a sudden start,' *ffrwd* = Ir. *sruth* 'stream,' etc. Here too I would put both πτάρ-νυ-μαι and πτύρω, in which (notwithstanding Curtius, 696) I venture to think that the πτ is not = the *st* of Lat. *sternuo, -sternare*, but comes regularly

---

² For the loss of *l* before *t* in Breton cf. *aut* 'ripa' = W. *allt* 'cliff,' Corn. *als* (gl. littus), Ir. *alt* (*alt in maro* 'the shore of the sea,' LU. 23b): *auten* 'rasorium' = Ir. *altain* (W. *ellyn*): *auter* 'altare' (W. *allor*): *faut* 'fissura' (W. *hollt*, spalt): *santer* = psalterium (W. *sallwyr*), etc. The modern *paotr* 'garçon' which Bopp, I think, compared with Skr. *putra*, is really for *paltr*, and connected with Eng. *paltry*, Low-Germ. *palt* 'lappen.'

from πċ, πj (Kuhn, Zeitschrift xi. 310), σπj, ΣΠ (Curtius, p. 683). The root SPAR-G (whence Lat. *spargo*) also seems to belong to this Number. From SPARG come W. *ffreuo* (ex SPREGAM) 'to gush,' 'to spout,' and *ffrocn,* Br. *froan* 'naris,' Ir. *srón* 'nasus' (ex SPROGNA).

No. 390. *σπλήν.* Br. *felch* 'rate,' 'splen,' Cath., is identical with Ir. *selg* ex **spelgâ,* the *g* becoming provected and then aspirated after the liquid, and the combination SP producing F according to rule in the British languages.

No. 391. Root *svap.* Here the initial *sv* has, as usual, given rise both to *s* and to *f* in Irish. The verbal forms *fiu* (= **fefup*) 'sopivit,' pl. *feótar* (= **fefupantar*), *foaid* (= **fupata-i*) 'sopiebat' Goidel². 87 n., deserve to be quoted : also *socht* (= **sop-to*) 'silence,' *sochtid* ¦' silet,' Corm. prull, *sochtais* 'siluit,' LU. 22b, to be compared with σιωπή (σι-σϜωπή), and the MHG. *swift* 'schweigend,' Fick 418. For the change of Indo-European *pt* to *ct* cf. *secht(n)* 'septem,' *necht* 'neptis.' The British forms W. *hun* 'sleep,' Corn. *fun* in *dy-fun* 'sleepless,' D. 2204, agree with the double form in Irish.

No. 393. The reflex of *ὑπαί,* as well as that of *ὑπό',* is found in Irish, namely *faoi-sin* .i. *fo no samhail sin* 'under or like that,' O'Cl. This form (spelt *foisin*) is found more than once in LU., e.g., *tanic in bliadain ass foisin,* 41a. So perhaps in Patrick's hymn : *cretim treodataid foisin oendata(i)d in dulemain dail* 'I believe in a Threeness, likewise a Oneness in the Creator of . . . .'

No. 395c. *βομβυλίς.* Add O.Ir. *bólcha* (gl. papulas), Parker 134.

No. 396. *βραχύς, brevis.* Compare W. *ber,* Br. *berr* 'brief,' Ir. *bearr* .i. *gairit,* Gl. 89, *cum-bair* 'brevis,' SM. .i. 182, *cum-bre* 'brevitas,' Z. 1050, *cuim-brigud* 'breviare,' Fél. Ep. 123 : perhaps Ir. *breagh* 'bellus,' O'Don. Gr. 74, anglicised 'braw.'

No. 400. W. *am,* Z. 674, keeps the original vowel of *ἀμφί,* etc.

No. 404. *ὑρφ-ανό-ς.* Add O.Ir. *ad-r-arbbai* 'he abolished, expunged or left out,' O'Don. Supp. (*arbai* = 'orbavit ?').

No. 405. *ὑ-φρύ-ς.* The Irish gen. dual *brúad* (I have never met the nom. sg.) occurs in the following passage from Lebor na huidre 113b, describing the hero Cúchulainn, *Atá limsa bá frass donemannaib rolád inachend. Dubithir leth dubfolach ecchtarde adá brúad deirgithir partaing a beoil,* thus rendered by Mr. Crowe : 'I should think it was a shower of pearls that was flung into his head. Blacker than the side of a black cooking-spit (?) was each of his two brows : redder than ruby his lips.' Another form *bra* or *brai* (cf. OHG. *bráwa*) .i. *mala* is given by O'Clery.

No. 406. O.Ir. *srub muicci* 'a swine's snout,' Corm. Tr. p. 154, is surely cognate with *sorbeo,* etc.

No. 407. Root φα. O.Ir. *ad-bo* .i. *urfocraim* 'I proclaim' .i. *obaim* 'prohibeo,' O'Dav. 50. To the secondary root *bhan* belong Ir. *at-boind* 'he proclaims,' 'inhibits,' O'Don. Supp., (cf. O.N. *banna,* OHG. *bannan* Fick² 809), 3d sg. pres. pass. *ad-bonnar urfogarthar,* O'Don. Supp. With φαληρός, φαλιός, and other words noticed under this Number the O.Ir. *beltine, beltene* is perhaps connected : with *bel* cf. O.N. *bál,* A.S. *bæl* 'flame :' the *tine, tene* is the same compound suffix that we have in *gel-tine* 'firewood,' Corm. fochonnad, and *cair-tine, cairddine* 'friendship,' Z. 777. The Greek φίγγος (ex *σπα-ν-γος) 'light' placed by Curtius under this Number cannot, I think, be separated from Skr. *pājas*, Lith. *spogalas* (Fick 413) and W. *ffaw* 'radiance' ex SPAGA. No. 410. Root φεν. Add O.W. *et-binam* (gl. lanio), Z. 1052, *du-ben-eticion* (gl. exsectis), Mart. Cap. 42 a.a., Br. *benaff* 'couper,' Cath. No. 412. Root φλα. Ir. *blor* (leg. *blór*) .i. *glor* 'noise,' O'Dav. 57, *blór* .i. *guth no glor*, O'Cl. belongs to the root φλυ. So the W. *blew* 'crines,' Z. 109, Corn. *bleu*, Br. *bleau, bleuenn.* No. 413. Root φρακ. The Ir. *bárc* .i. *iomad* 'a multitude,' O'Cl., is cognate with Lat. *farcio, frequens* here cited. No. 414. φράτηρ. Add O.W. *braut*, Corn. *braud* vel *broder.* No. 415. φρέαρ. As the Ir. *tipra* is an ant-stem, the ground-form cannot be *do-ad-bravat*, as Windisch conjectures. I know not whether the verbs *do-e-prannat* (gl. alluant), Ml. 39d, *toi-prinnit* (gl. influunt), Goidel². 70, *do-r-e-prend-set* (emicuerunt) *ib.*, *do-n-e-prenn-et* (gl. quo . . . liquefiunt), Sg. 209b, are connected with Goth. *brunna*, but phonetically the connection is possible, for the Irish *p* is here a *b* provected by the lost *th* of the preposition *aith*, Z. 880. No. 417. Root φυ. Ir. *both*, Corn. *bos* = Lith. *búta-s* 'house.' Ir. *bot* 'penis,' O'Don. Sup., = *but-va* (cf. *fu-tu-o*). The Ir. *bíthe* (.i. *bannda* ' femininus,' O'Cl.) suggests that the Lat. *fēmina* should be transferred to this Number from No. 307. Ir. *budh* .i. *bioth no sáoghal*, O'Cl., may also come from the root *bhu.* No. 419. Ir. *einech* = Old-Corn. (?) and Br. *enep* 'face,' Z. 838, 1060, should surely be compared with the Skr. *anika*, Zend *ainika* here cited. No. 421. ἀνά. Cf. the intensive prefix *an-, en-* in Corn. *an-auhel* (gl. procella), W. *en-awel*, Br. *am-pref-an, am-poeson* 'rubeta,' Ir. *an-fad* 'storm.' No. 422. ἀ-νήρ. Add W. *nerth*, O.W. *nerthheint* (gl. armant), Juv. 89. No. 424. ἔνεκ. The root NANK is in O.Ir. *coim-nac-mar* 'potuimus,' and other forms, Z. 451. The root ANK is in Ir. *t-ic, tair-ic* 'venit,' *t-anac r-anac* 'veni,' M.Br. *di-ano* 'deviare,' Cath., Ir. *tecm-ang* (gl. fors), *agad* (gl. fors), *tocad* (gl. fors), *do-thoicdib* (gl. fatis). No. 425. ἐνί, antar. Add O.W. *permed-intcredou* (gl. ilia), Juv. 35 : Corn. *enederen* (gl. exstum), O.W. *ithr*, Beitr. vii. 398 = *inter*. No. 428. ἔνος. Add O.W. *hencassou* (gl. monimenta), Juv. 49. No. 429. Add to the derivatives from the root MAN O.Ir. *taith-met* 'commemoratio,' Fél. Ep. 131,235, *foimtiu, toimtiu* 'opinio,' Z. 42. With the roots μαθ, *madh*, the Ir. *modh* .i. *fear* 'vir' and *modh* .i. *obair* 'opera,' O'Cl., seem connected. No. 430. ναῦς. Add *noere* 'nautas,' O'Cl. No. 431. Root νεμ. Add Ir. *nemed* (gl. sacellum), Gaulish *nanto* (gl. valle), Beitr. vi. 229. No. 432. Ir. *nett*, gen. *nit*, Goidel². 84, W. *nyth* 'nest,' ex *netto-s, *nes-to-s, *nes-do-s*, No. 355, may, like Lat. *nidus* ex *nis-dus*, be cognate with *va(σ)ίω*. No. 435. If we may assume that *áru* (gl. rien), Z. 264, a fem. *n*-stem, W. *aren*, has lost initial *n* (like Ir. *Uachongbail, escu, escongan* 'eel,' *ess* 'weasel,'

Br. *effou* 'cieulx,' *azr*—now *aer*—*Ormant, Ormandi*) we might equate it with the Old-Latin **nefro* pl. *nefrones* 'testiculi' Festus, s. v. *nefrendes*, and thus connect it with OHG. *niero*, Gr. νεφρός.

No. 443. Root *rv, σνν*. To this Number belong Ir. *snuadh* .i. *sruth* 'flumen,' O'Cl., *snuad* 'cæsaries,' Corm., W. *di-nëu* 'to pour,' Br. *di·nou* 'fondre.' From root SNA, come Lat. *nare, natrix* 'water-snake' = Ir. *nathir* (gen. *nathrach* a fem. *c*-stem), W. *neidr*. In the Ir. *snob* (gl. suber) Sg. 64, *snamach* (gl. suber), Ir. Gl. 391, W. *nawf* 'a swim,' Ir. *ro-sná* .i. *dorinne snámh*, O'Cl., the *s* is preserved.

No. 448. ὦνος. The O.Ir. *uain (oc-uain* 'in commodando,' Z. 634) is= ὠνή, *vasna·m*. The Irish *oin* .i. *iasacht* 'loan,' O'Cl., O'Dav. 109, is certainly cognate with ὀνίνημι here cited. The W. *echwyn (e-chwyn ? cch-wyn ?)* is obscure to me.

No. 449. Ir. *samud* 'congregation,' Br. h. 13, *saim* 'yoke,' Corm., *sét* 'instar' (ex *sam-ta*), Fél. June 16, *samh* in the phrase *samh-lat* .i. *amail tu*, O'Cl., and O.W. *amal* 'ut,' Juv. 32, are all cognate with ἅμα.

No. 449b. ἀμάω, *meto*. Add O.W. *et-met* 'retonde,' Juv. 77.

No. 453. ἡμι-. Add the W. *hauter* 'half' ex SAM-ter, and the Ir. privative particle *am*-, Z. 860.

No. 459. Root μαχ. Ir. *mactadh* .i. *marbhadh* 'a killing,' O'Cl., seems to belong to this Number.

No. 461. Root με. Add O.Ir. *methos* .i. *crich* 'a boundary,' Corm., dat. sg. *methus*, Corm. Tr. p. 109 ; from the extended root ME-N, we have O.W. *menntaul* (gl. bilance), M. Cap. 12 b, and *montol* 'trutina,' Z. 1054 ; from the further extended root *MEN-S* we have *tomus* 'mensura' (= *do-fo-MENS-u*), O.W. *do-guo-misur*[*am*] (gl. geo), Z. 1052 : Ir. *mesurda* (gl. modicum), Ir. Gl. No. 807, *mesraigthe* (gl. modestus), Z. 780. With the Old-Lat. *mānus* here cited compare the Ir. *muin* 'good' (*adfenar olcc anmuinib, adfenar maith muinib* 'which renders evil to the ungood, which renders good to the good,' SM. i. 256).

No. 462. The Ir. *magh* in *magh-lorg* .i. *mór-lorg*, O'Cl., is identical with μέγας. The Ir. *maighne* .i. *mór* 'magnus' points to an Old-Celtic **magnio*.

No. 467. Root μερ. Compare Ir. *mir*, W. *mèr* 'particle.'

No. 469. μέσσος for μεθjος. The prefix *mid*- occurs in at least four Old-Irish words : *mid-chuairt* 'mid-court,' Fél. Ep. 94, *mid-lái* 'of mid-day,' LU. 78a, *mid-nocht* 'mid-night,' Reeves, *Culdees*, 86, *im-mid-ais* 'in middle age,' LB. 71, lower margin. In H. 2. 16, col. 119 *leth* 'half' glosses *mid*.

No. 472. μήτηρ. The Gaulish dat. pl. *matrebo* of the inscription of Nimes might have been quoted here.

No. 473. μῆχος. Add Ir. *mám* .i. *cumas* 'potestas,' O'Cl. Whether Ir. *mám* 'jugum,' Z. 17, *com-mám* .i. *bean* 'uxor,' O'Cl., *com-mamsa* 'matrimonii,' O'Dav. 70, belong to this Number, I do not venture to say. They are apparently cognate with OHG. *gi-mahhā* 'uxor,' 'conjux,' O.N. *māg-r*, Goth. *mēg-s*, which Fick². 828 brings from the European root *MAG* = Indo-Germ. *MAGH*.

No. 474. Root μιγ, μίσγω. The Old-Irish *cummasc* 'mixtio' (not 'commutatio '), whence *cummascthai* 'promiscua,' Z. 182, stands for **cum-mesc*, the vocalic sequence *u-e* regularly becoming *u-a* : cf. asluat, druad, Samual, toddiusgat from *asluet, *drued, Samuel, *toddiusget. There is therefore no ground for Windisch's conjecture ' *cummasc* ..... scheint des Vocals wegen abzuliegen.'

No. 476. O.Ir. *moth* ' nomen virili membro,' Corm., belongs to the root MAT, whence μόθος, mathāmi, möndull, me-n-tula, etc.

No. 485. ὄμβρος. Add O.Ir. *amor* ' a tub,' Corm. Trans. 15 : the Gaulish river-name *Ambris* and W. *Ambir* are put by Glück (Neue Jahrbücher, 1864, p. 601) with ὄμβρος, etc. Gaulish *ambe* (gl. rivo), *inter-ambes* (gl. inter rivos), Beitr. vi. 229.

No. 488. Root ἀρ. Add Ir. *comh-al no ac-comh-al* .i. *coimhcheangal*, O'Cl., *acom-al-tae* ' conjunctus,' Z. 479, ad-com-l-atar, Z. 473, arm or airm in airm-gein .i. amra gein .i. gein mhaith ' marvellous birth,' ' a good birth,' O'Cl.

No. 490. ἀρόω. Add *arinca* ' frumenti genus Gallicum,' Plin.

No. 491. O.Ir. *eirr* (gl. curruum princeps) Goidel². 57, gen. *erred* ' champion ' is cognate with ἄρσην, the rs becoming rr as in err = ars, tarrach ex *tarsāco root TARS, etc.

No. 492. Add O.Ir. *rám* ' remus,' W. rhaw ' shovel.'

No. 493. Ir. *briathar*, a fem. ā-stem, is = Ρρήτρα, VR becoming BR as often. The Skr. *brū* ' to speak ' = Zend mrū here cited seems to occur in the Ir. fris-brudi ' renuit,' Ml. 44b, Goidel². 40, and O'Clery's frioth-bruth .i. diultadh ' negatio,' and in the British co-brouol (gl. verbialia), Z. 1065.

No. 496. εἶρος, vellus. Ir. *folt*, W. *gwallt* ' hair ' also come from the root VAR ' decken.' Hence too Ir. *fearn* .i. sgiath ' shield,' O'Cl. So perhaps Ir. *ulaidh* .i. srathar ' packsaddle,' O'Cl.

No. 499. εὐρύς. The Ir. *ferr* = W. *guell* ' better ' = variyas. The positive may be in the Old-Celtic names Veru-cloetius (Εὐρυκλῆς, cloetius, like κλειτός from root CLU ?) and Veru-lamium.

No. 500. Root ὁρ, orior. The O.Ir. *aur-ur-as* ' cursura,' Goidel². 32, com-thur-ur-as ' incursus ' (com-du-air-Uk-asta), Z. 887, belong to this. Hence too the common word turas (= do-ur-asta) ' iter,' ' peregrinatio.'

No. 501. Root Fορ. The Ir. *aire* ' vigilance ' (now *faire* with prosthetic f, O'Don. Gr. 327) has lost initial v (f), like olann for *folann : fili ' poet ' seems cognate with W. gwelwr ' seer,' as Ir. filis (.i. seallais ' vidit,' O'Cl.) is = W. gwelas. The W. guarai (gl. scena), Z. 1056, may also be added.

No. 502. ὀρ-μή. Add O.Ir. *sel* in the phrase cach-'la-sel . . . in sel aile ' modo . . . modo,' Z. 560.

No. 503. ὄρνις, Lith. erēlis. Add W. eryr ' eagle,' also crydd.

No. 505. Ir. *err* ' tail ' (from *erso) LL. cited Rev. Celt. i. 258, is certainly = ὄρρος, OHG. ars ' anus.' See at No. 491.

No. 510. O.W. *di-di-oul-am*, gl. micturio (not ' glisco '), Z. 136, 1052, like O.Ir. *fual*, is cognate with οὖρον, and this Welsh form supports Windisch's theory that the f in f-ual is prosthetic. The original r seems kept in Ir. ferath ' humor ' (ocuturgabail fri fual ocus ferath ' raising thee up from water and wet,' O'Curry, Manners and Customs iii. 375) = W. guyraut ' liquor,' Corn. gwyras, Z. 842, 843. So in the O.Ir. -fera ' pluit ' (ni fera cid oen *banne*, Z. 952), *ferais* 'pluvit' (*ferais anmich* 'it poured with rain [a],' Brocc. h. 30, *ferais snechta mór forru* 'a great snow showered upon them,' Táin LU.), *forthain* 'shower,' and *diorain* (*di-for-ani*) .i. *snigheadh no siledh fearthana no fleachaidh* 'the dropping of a shower or of moisture,' O'Cl. So perhaps in *foirthiu* (gl. marmora), Tur. 65.

No. 511. W. *erf-in-en* (O.W. *erb-in-enu*) is, I think, cognate with ὄάφυς. The modern Irish *raib* seems only a loan from Lat. *rāpa*.

No. 523b. Root *ἀλ, alo*. Add O.Ir. *ail* 'esca,' Z. 527.

No. 527. Root *Fελ, volvo*. Add Ir. *fillim (ll* ex *lv)* 'flecto,' Z. 983n.

No. 529. ἔλαφος. O.Ir. *elit* 'doc,' Corm. Tr. 68, W. *elain* 'hind' belong to this Number. Pictet's *arr* 'hirsch' belongs either to No. 491, or to OIIG. *far* 'taurus' ex *fars*, No. 376.

No. 536b. W. *lleibio, llepio* 'to lick,' and Br. *lipat* point to a root LAP. But W. *llyfu* points to a root LAB or LABII.

No. 540. *Losc* .i. *bacach* 'claudus,' Corm. Tr. 104, acc. pl. *luscu*, Fiacc's h. 34, is identical with λοξός, Lat. *luxus*. So *lesc* = *luxus*.

No. 544. With Latin *glis* (stem *glit*) I would connect the Irish *lestar* 'vas,' Z. 166, W. *llestr*, from *lit-tro*. With ὑ(σ)λιβ-ρο'ς and OIIG. *slëffar* (lubricus) the Irish *slemon*, Z. 776, (ex *slib-no*), W. *llyfn* 'smooth,' 'sleek' are probably cognate.

No. 545. *Libhearn* .i. *clann no crodh* 'children or goods,' O'Cl., is cognate with the Lat. *libet, liber* here cited. The nom. pl. occurs in a note to the *Amra Choluimchille* (LU.) :—

Nech frisbert athigerna	" Whoso hath betrayed his lord,
nirbu(t) ile a liberna	His children will not be many.
corrucait namait achend	May foes carry off his head,
agabair is adubcend [b].	His steed and his sword ! "

No. 546. λύω. The Old-Welsh *lou* 'louse' in *leu-esice* (gl. cariantem), Beitr. vii. 388, now *lleu-en*, pl. *llau*, Br. *louenn* 'pediculus,' like the German *laus*, belongs to the root LU.

No. 547. λῦμα, λούω. The Gaulish *lautro* (gl. balneo), Beitr. vi. 229, should be equated with λούω. So M.Br. *louazr* 'alveus,' *loet* 'mucidus,' *loedaff* 'mucidare,' Cath. The Ir. *lunae* 'to wash,' O'Don. Supp., and *con-luan* .i. *cac na con* 'dogs' dung,' *ib.*, are also connected with the words here cited.

No. 548. λύγξ. Ir. *loisi* .i. *sionnaigh* 'foxes,' O'Cl., seems cognate with the OHG. *luhs* 'luchs' here cited.

No. 549. Root (σ)λυγ. Add the O.W. *ro-luncas* (gl. gutturicavit), Br. *loncaff* 'englouter,' Ir. *longadh* .i. *caitheamh* 'consumptio,' O'Cl.

---

[a] Cf. the Latin *lacte pluisse*. Here *ánmich* is the dat. sg. of *ánmech* (O'Clery's *ainbheach* .i. *deura iomdha no fearthain* 'plenteous tears or a shower'), gen. *ánbige*, Brocc. h. 33, a fem. ā-stem : cf. the use of the datives *ceill* and *biuth*, Z. 917, 918.
[b] AMRA, ed. Crowe, p. 56, where this easy quatrain is mistranslated. It is cited by O'Clery s. v. *frismbeart*, where O'Clery (thinking of the Latin *liburna*) renders *libhearna* by *longa* 'galleys.' O'Clery explains *ni-r-but* by *narab* 'ne sit : " but it is a future (= *ní* + *ropat, rubat* 'erunt,' Z. 498), not an imperative.

No. 569. *Ισος, vishu* . Cf. Ir. *fiu* (ex **visu*) .i. *cosmail* 'similis,' O'Cl.

No. 571. Root *σα*. The Ir. *síl*, W. *hil* : W. *had* 'seed,' Br. *hadaff* 'serère' may be added to *sēmen, saian* and the other derivatives here mentioned.

No. 574. *σύβη*. The Ir. *fobhaidh* .i. *luath no ésgaidh* 'swift or nimble,' O'Cl. and perhaps the W. *chwaf* (ex **svaba-*) 'a gust,' 'instantly,' seem connected with the words here cited.

No. 577. Root *strang, strag*. The Ir. *sreang, sreangaim* here cited are genuine words, though probably taken by Pictet from O'Reilly, *srengais* 'traxit,' LU. 26a, *sreangadh* .i. *tarraing (do-air-sraing)* 'tractio,' O'Cl. The root *strag* has in Irish lost the *s* : *tracht* (ex **trag-ta, *stragta*) .i. *neart* 'strength,' O'Cl., *rith tar tracht* 'running beyond strength,' O'Don. Supp., *dí-thraicht* .i. *aimhneartmhar* 'strengthless,' O'Cl.

No. 579. *σύς*. With this the Ir. *socc* (in *socc-sáil*, gl. loligo, Z. 30) = W. *hwch*, Corn. *hoch*, Br. *houch*, seems cognate. Grimm's theory of a borrowing here by Celts from Germans (Eng. *hog*, NHG. *haksch*, Beitr. ii. 175) is overturned by the Irish form with *s*.

No. 582. *ἄξων*. Add W. *echel* 'axle,' Br. *ahel*.

No. 583. *αὔξω*. O.Ir. *ásaim*, Mid. Ir. *f-ásaim* ' cresco ' = *vakshâmi*.

No. 584. *ἔξ*. The O.Ir. *fes* in *mórfeser* 'a heptad of persons,' Z. 313, lit. ' a great hexad,' *mor-fesser* LU. 21a, dat. sg. *morfessiur*, Fél. July 18, should have been cited, as well as the forms beginning with *s*. See Windisch, Kuhn's Zeitschrift xxi. 428.

No. 585. *αἴές*. In the Ir. *étte* .i. *aois* ' ætatis,' *aos éta* .i. *daoine aosda* 'aged persons,' O'Cl., we probably have another instance of the assimilation of *s* to a following *t* noticed above at No. 355.

No. 586. The Irish reflex of the Zend *av* ' to protect ' *au-dio* and other words here cited is in the third sg. pres. *-ó ,-ói ,-óei* or *-ai*, all meaning 'servat.' Examples are numerous : *ni-m-ó do-legend-so* 7 *ni-m-chobrathar-side* 'non me servat lectio tua (sacrarum literarum) neque me hæc adiutat,' Goidel². 180, (where it is wrongly rendered), *dobeir dig con-ói ríg dogni echt* ' dat potionem quæ servat regem facinus committentem,' LU. 98a, *con-n-oi* 'qui servat,' Z. 431, *co-ta-óei* 'servat id,' *ib.*, *for-ta-com-ai-som* 'servat id ille,' *ib.* So O'Clery : *connáoi* .i. *coimhédaidh no cumdaighidh* : 3d sg. pret. *con-r-óeth biu bath* ' is qui servavit vitam mortuus est.' Amra Chol. LU. 8b.: 3rd pl. pret. *con-r-oitatar*, Rev. Celt. i. 74, Passive *co-tam-r-oither (cotamroether B.)* 'sine ut servor,' Fél. Ep. 69. The Welsh reflex of *au-di-o* is *ewi* ' to listen.' We can hardly separate the Bret. *couel* (ex **avelo*) ' voluntas,' Cath., from the Lat. *av-i-dus* here noticed.

No. 587. Root *àF. āω*. Add Corn. *anawhel* (gl. procella), W. *enawel*. As to the prefix see No. 421.

No. 589. *ἔαρ*. Add O.W. *guiannuin* (gl. vere) ex **visanténa-*. See Beitr. vii. 235. In the Irish *errach* for **(v)esráca*, initial *v* has been lost, as in the following :—

> *aire* ' heed,' OHG. *wara* ' consideratio,' ' cura,'
> *ásaim* ' I wax,' *asait clanda* ' crescunt plantæ,' II. 2. 16, col. 90,
> *ess* ' bos,' W. *ych*, pl. *ychen* = Goth. *auhsa* from **vexan*,

ét-ach ' ves-ti-s,' *étiud* = *vestitus,*
olann (W. *gulan*) ' wool,' *vellus,*
orc, org ' cædere' (*orcun* 'occisio,' Z. 738), (*F*)ράκος, *F*ρήγ-νυ-μι,
oss ' cervus ' = Skr. *vasta* 'goat,'
remmad ' distortio,' ῥέμβω, ῥόμβος, *(v)rengvātu*, A.S. *vringan.*

Both *guiannuin* and *errach*, like the Latin subst. *vernum*, may have been
originally adjectives used with some word equivalent to ' tempus ' : cf. Lucr.
v. 802 ' ova relinquebant, exclusæ tempore verno.'

No. 593. With *iría, vi-men, vitex*, etc., the following Celtic words are
cognate : Ir. *fiamh* .i. *slabhradh* ' chain,' O'Cl., Ir. *féith* (gl. fibra), Z. 19, W.
gwden, Corn. *guiden* (gl. cutulus, *i. e.* catulus ' a kind of fetter ').

No. 595. ὄϊς, *ovis.* Another form of O.I. *ói* is in the masc. *ia*-stem
ae-gaire ' shepherd,' where *-gaire* (also in *in-gaire*), like the 3rd sg. pret. *ar-gair-t*,
Brocc. h. 33, is to be compared with ἀ-γείρω from *σα-γερ-ίω, NHG. *kehren*,
A.S. *cordhor* ' heerde,' ' schaar.' To connect ἀμνός with ὄϊς, though phonetically possible (cf. σεμνός) is doubtful. Where then would be the Greek
reflex of *agnus* ? 'Αμνός, *agnus*, Slav. *agnǐcǐ*, and the Irish diminutival ending
in *-án*[a] all go together : ἀμνός ex *άβνος, *άγνος, Fick, *Spracheinheit* 53,
where, however, these words are erroneously connected with Ir. *uan* ' lamb,'
which (like W. *oen*) is = Lith. *avina* ' wether.'

No. 602. Root *i, si.* Add Ir. *sin* .i. *muince* ' monile,' II. 3, 18, p. 73,
col. 3, *sion* (= *sinn*) .i. *idh no slabhradh* ' collar or chain,' O'Cl., *sinann* .i.
slabradh, II. 3, 18, p. 17.

No. 603. The locative of the pronominal stem *sa* occurs with the
suffixed demonstrative *na* (cf. Lat. *si-c*) in the O.Ir. adverb *sin* .i. *as amhlaidh*,
O'Cl., who cites *IS sin téid an mal in a theach righ* ' thus the king went
into his palace.'

No. 604. Root *ú.* O.Ir. *suth* .i. *lacht* ' milk,' *ont-suth* .i. *on loimm*, Corm.
s. v. *nth*, *suba* .i. *fuil* ' blood,' LU. 50a. *Sabrann* (the name of the river Lee
near Cork) = W. *Hafren*, *Sabrina* (*br* ex *vr*), Gaulish *Savara*, la *Sèvre*
(Pictet) are all from the root *su* here noticed.

No. 605. υιός. Root *su.* Add the O.Ir. *too, toud* ' gignere,' O'Cl.,
(= *do-soo, *do-soud*) : *fuil nuitlige iar too* ' the blood of a cow after calving,'
ib., 3d sg. pret. *gur-thoi* .i. *go rug* ' genuit,' O'Cl.

No. 608. ὑσμῖν-. The O.Ir. *iodna* ' arms,' Petrie's *Tara* 166, whence
the adj. *iodhnach* .i. *armach no cathach*, O'Cl., and the O.W., Corn. and Br.
iud, the first element of many proper names of men, are cognate with Skr.
yudh-ma. Other instances of the preservation of the semivowel in Irish are
iúg (= *iudic-*) in *iúg-suide* (gl. tribunal), Z. 183, and *iunad* gen. *iunta* ' coitus
(avium),' O'Don. Supp., which seems derived from the root *yu* ' jungere.'

---

[a] This is the Old-Celtic *agnos*, of which the gen. sg. *-agni* frequently occurs on the
Irish Oghom inscriptions, e. g. *Mailagni, Talagni, Ulccagni.* The last word is = *Olcdin*, cf.
Gaulish VLKOS, Rev. Num. 1861, p. 344, and perhaps Skr. *ulká* ' meteor,' ' firebrand.'
VLCAGNVS, the nom. sg. of Ir. *Ulccagni*, occurs (according to Mr. Rhys) on the Welsh
stone at Llanfihangel-ar-arth. *Maglagni* (= the Ir. *Mailagni !*) occurs on the Llaufechan
stone.

No. 613. The Ir. *áir* in *an-áir* 'ab oriente,' Z. 611, appears related to ἤρι, ἤριος, ἄριστον. (So Goth. *air*, O.N. *ár.*) That these words belong to the root US, VAS, seems improbable. But with this root I would connect Ir. *fáir* 'dawn,' Corm. = W. *gwawr* = Skr. *vāsara* 'day.' No. 620. Root *ϝεπ*, VAK. Add the following Irish words from O'Clery : *foch-t* .i. *iarfaighi(dh)* 'quæstio ;' *fuighcall* .i. *briathar* 'verbum ;' *fuchain* .i. *foeighemh no glaodh* 'monitio vel clamor ;' *fa-n-g* .i. *fiach* 'corvus.' The form *fiach* 'corvus' is from **véco*, root *vec (vic ?*), to which Curtius refers Lat. *convīcium, in-vi(c)-tare.*

No. 628. ὀπός, *sucus.* In O.W. *dis-suncnetic* (gl. exanclata 'pumped out, sucked out'), Mart. Cap. 3. a. a., the *s* of the root SVAK is preserved. In other Welsh words (*chwaeth* ex **svahta* 'savour,' 'taste,' *chwey* 'sweet' ex **sveka*) the combination *sv* has regularly become *hv, chw.*

No. 630. Root *πεπ.* Other British words from the root PAK are W. *poeth,* Br. *poaz* = πεπτός, Br. *poazat* 'coquere.' The Ir. *coice* 'coquus' and *cucenn* 'coquina' are apparently loans.

No. 631. Ir. *can* .i. *tan no úair,* O'Cl. = Goth. *hvan,* Eng. *when,* should be added. With ἐ-κεῖ, *ci-s, ci-tra* mentioned in the note to this Number I would connect the Ir. *cé* (used in the phrase *for bith chê* 'on this world,' *cen-* in *cen-alpande* 'cisalpinus,' Z. 870, *cen-tar* 'pars citerior' and *cen-tarach* (gl. citimus, gl. citra), Z. 72, 781.

No. 632. Root *σεπ.* The Old-Welsh *hep, hepp* 'inquit' occurs often in the Capella Glosses, and should be cited in preference to the Mediæval Welsh *heb.* The Ir. *aithescc,* Z. 67, 'answer' (**ati-s-co-*) and *tairme-scc,* Z. 67, 'prohibitio,' not 'perturbatio,' **tarmi-s-co* should be added.

No. 634. Root *βα.* Add Ir. *béim* .i. *céim* 'step,' O'Cl. The Lat. *vādere* here cited may come from **va-n-dere* = Ir. *fonnadh* .i. *foghluasacht no siubhal* 'moving or travelling,' O'Cl., just as *vācillare* from *vancillare,* Schmidt, Vocalismus 104. Anyhow *vādo* cannot be separated from *vadan.*

No. 640. W. *bwyd,* Br. *boet* 'cibus' = βίοτος.

No. 643. Root *βορ.* Ir. *broth* 7 *bruith* .i. *feoil* 'caro,' O'Cl., gen. *bruithe,* also belong to this Number, the *br* coming from *vr* as often. And the old *g* appears in *for-diu-guilsiter* (gl. vorabuntur), Ml. 84, *fordiucailsi* 'absorpti,' Ml. 59, and other such forms, Goidel⸳., 25, *fordiuglantaid* 'devorator,' O'Mulc. Gl. No. 780 and in *gleith* .i. *caitheamh,* O'Cl.

No. 651. Root θερ. With *ghransa-s* 'sonnengluth' here cited, and perhaps χρυσός, I would connect a number of Irish words with *s* ex *ns* :—*gris* 'fire,' O'Don. Supp., *grisach* 'burning ember,' etc. Words like **gris* 'fire' (*gristaitnem na gréne,* O'Don. Gr. 286), with short *i,* for **grid-ti,* seem connected with χλιδή, χλίω, A.S. *glitan,* etc. Hence *gresuim* 'incito,' 'excito.' The O.Ir. *gronn* and *gorn* 'firebrand,' Corm., are also from the root *ghar.*

No. 652. The Welsh *ffwn* 'breath' (Gen. vii. 22, Dan. x. 17), *ffwn* 'a puff,' 'sigh,' (ex SPUNA) support Curtius' theory that φῦσα and the other words here cited come from a root SPU.

No. 653. With ἄφ-νος, *opes,* the Irish gen. pl. *innan-ane* 'divitiarum,' Z. 1035, dat. pl. *donaib ánib,* Z. 1028, acc. pl. *anu,* Z. 240, seem cognate.

No. 651. Add the following from O'Clery: *bugh* .i. *briscadh* 'fractio,' *buich* .i. *briscadh, com-bocht* .i. *dobris* 'fregit.'

No. 655. Ir. *braigim* 'pedo,' *bruach* (gl. margo), Z. 22, seem cognate with *fra-n-go, brikan.* With (*F*)ρήγ-νυ-μι, Ir. *failghis* .i. *buailis no dobhris* 'perculit vel fregit,' O'Cl., seems cognate.

No. 656. Root ἀλ. The Ir. *salt* .i. *léim* 'a leap,' Corm., is possibly not a loan. It occurs in Irish topography. *So-alt* (i. e. *so-salt*) .i. *soiléim* .i. *léim maith* 'a good leap,' O'Clery, who also has *alt* .i. *léim.*

No. 657. ἅλς. Ir. *sál* 'sea' should be added. It occurs in the Book of Leinster, fo. 19. a. 2 :—

In-tocéb mo-curchan ciar	'Shall I launch my black skiff .
for-inn-ocian n-uchtlethan n-án	On the ocean broad-breasted, splendid?
in-rag a-rí richid réil	Shall I go, O King of bright heaven,
as-mo-thoil fein ar-in-sál [a].	According to my own desire, on the sea ?'

The gen. sg. *sáil* seems to occur in *socc-sáil* (gl loligo), Z. 30, where the *ái* (an infected *á*) is, wrongly, I think, treated as a diphthong.

No. 658. βλάστη. O.Ir. *bra-n-d, brann* in *od-brann* (gl. talus), Goidel[c]. 57, is, I think with Nigra *Gl. Taur.* 63, from the root VARDH : cf. Skr. *bradhna* in *çata-bradhna* 'hundred-pointed,' A.S. *brant* 'high.' So Ir. *brú* gen. *bronn* 'venter,' Z. 264 and *bruinne* 'mamma,' 'pectus,' acc. pl. *bruinniu,* Z. 653.

~~No. 659. Root βαλ. Ir. *ferr* 'better,' W. *gwell* (= Skr. *variyas*) should be added.~~

No. 660. Root *Γελ,* Skr *var.* Many Irish words belong to this Number : *félma* (gl. sæpes), Z. 770, *fál* 'hedge,' Z. 953, SM. i. 236, *foil* .i. *tech* 'house' (*mucc-foil* gl. stabulum porcorum, Z. 183), *fola* .i. *brat* 'cloak,' O'Cl. etc.

No. 663. Root SVAR. The O.Ir. *selam* .i. *neam* 'heaven,' (Lebar Lecain Glossary, No. 301) is cognate with σέλας, *ser-enus,* &c. ; so also *sellad* or *silled* 'to see,' *sellach* 'eyewitness,' SM. i. 240, *sella* 'eyes,' T. B. Fr , where *ll = ly, ry* as in "Ελλη = **svaryá* (Kuhn). So perhaps in *aislinge* 'a vision,' **ad-sell-ang-ia,* Corm. Tr. 13. The forms εἴλη (ex *i-Fελη*?), (*F*)αλέα here cited seem rather to belong to a root VAR or UR whence Skr. *ulká* 'meteor,' 'firebrand,' *ulmuka* 'brand' Fick[c]. 182), W. *ulw* 'ashes,' 'cinders,' O.Ir. *ar-ul loscas tene,* Z. 949.

No. 664. Root σκαλ. Ir. *scailt* 'a cleft,' *ro-ceachladar* (leg. *ro-che-chl-atar*) .i. *dotho-chladar* 'fodierunt,' O'Cl., *forroichlaid (*fo-ro-ce-chlaid)* gl.

---

[a] This is misquoted and the verbs are mistranslated in O'Curry's *Manners and Customs of the Ancient Irish* iii. 388. But this is nothing to a passage in the preceding page, where a prose proverb (*maraith sercc céin mardda aithne a máellecán* 'manet amor quamdiu maneut opes, O M.' Nigra, *Rel. Celt.* 22) is printed as verse and translated thus : " "Twas my much-loved long-coveted treasure, to understand their warbling." Take another specimen from the same book : King Conchobar, in the *Táin bó Cualnge,* after seeing the feats of the boy Cúchulainn, says regretfully, 'If (only) he had (i. e. could perform) the deeds of championship, even as he hath the boy-deeds!' *Nicumdas arád, ar Fergus, feib atré in mac bec atresat a gnima óclachais leis,* LL. 47 a. 2. " It is not meet to say that ;" says Fergus ; "as the little boy will grow (literally 'rise') up, his deeds of championship will grow up with him." O'Curry (ii. 362) renders this easy passage thus: " It is not proper to speak so," said Fergus, "for according to the manner in which the little boy has performed his actions, (it is clear) he must (already) know the feats of championhood."

effodit, Ml. 24c, *focechlaitis* .i. *rotochlaidis*, Transcript of Laws by O'Curry 2044, *claide* 'ditch' = W. *cladd*, Br. *cleuz*.

Having thus suggested addenda to most of Curtius' Numbers [a], I will now mention some of the phonetic changes in which the Neo-Celtic languages resemble Greek. Windisch, *Grundzüge*, pp. 394, 415, notices the regular Welsh, Cornish and Breton change of initial *s* before a vowel to *h*. But there are many more :—

1°. The weakening of a vowel-flanked tenuis to a media, which we find in ἀρήγω, κραυγή, ᾽Αρτέμιδος (= Doric ᾽Αράμιτος), καλύβη, and other words cited by Curtius, pp. 522—530. This is the rule in the British languages.

2°. The loss of *s* in the combinations σρ, σν, σμ, Curtius, p. 681. This is common in Welsh : cf. *rhes* with Ir. *sreth* 'series ;' *nedd* 'nit,' *nawdd* 'protection,' *nawf* 'a swim,' *noden* 'thread,' *notuid* 'needle,' with Ir. *sned, snádud, snám, snáthe, snáthat;* cf. too W. *nyddu*, Br. *nezaff* 'filer' with (σ)νήθω and ἔννη (nebat) ex ἴ-σνη; W. *mwg* = Ir. *múch* (*ainm dileas do dheataigh* 'a name proper to smoke,' O'Cl.), Br. *moguel*, with σμύχω for *σμύκω, Fick 416; Ir. *much* .i. *toirse* 'tristitia,' O'Cl., with ἐπι-σμυγ-ερός; W. *mynawyd* 'awl' with σμινύη.

3°. The change of ν to μ before the labial nasal (ΤΕΜ ΜΥΣΙΑΝ, ΤΩΜ ΜΙΣΘΩΣΕΩΝ, Curtius, p. 532): cf. O.Ir. *am-mag*, Z. 214, *innam-miled, innam-moge*, Z. 216.

4°. The hardening of a medial by a following spiritus asper (Curtius, p. 425), as in ἄνθος *ant-h-os* = Skr. *and-h-as*. So the Old-Irish article (*s*)*ind* becomes (*s*)*int* wherever infected *s* (= *h*) follows [b], Beitr. i., Z. 44. So the preposition *ind* (Gaulish *ande*) becomes *int* before infected *s*, Z. 878. So in the preposition *imb* = ἀμφί the *b* changes into *p* before infected *s* : *impu* = *imb-su, impod* = *imb-sód*, etc. So the *b* of *lebaid* 'bed,' gen. *leptha*, becomes *p* before *th*, pronounced *h*. A like phenomenon is the change into *f* (or *ph*) of the *v*-sound when followed by *th* (pronounced *h*): *dephthigim* 'dissideo,' Z. 62, a denominative from *debuith*, where the vowel-flanked *b* is infected. So in Modern Ir. *foirfe* = O.Ir. *foirbthe* (*foirvthe*) 'perfectus.'

5°. The change of ρj, λj to ρρ, λλ, Curtius, p. 652, is paralleled by the Ir. *ferr* 'better,' = W. *gwell* = Skr. *variyas*, and by the W. *pell* 'far' ex *peljo-s* = πειραῖος, and *oll, arall* = Ir. *uile, araile* (Rhys).

6°. As regards the generation of parasitic sounds, the British languages afford four interesting parallels to Greek : first, in the change to *p*, through the intermediate stage *kv*, of the *K* corresponding with Skr. and Zend *k, ch*, Greek (κϜ) κ, κκ, π, ππ, τ, ττ, Lat. *qv, c* (see Fick, *Spracheinheit* 6, 7, 62); secondly, in the growth of *v* to *gv* (Curtius, pp. 584, 586) both in anlaut and inlaut (*nequid* 'novus,' Ir. *og* 'ovum'); thirdly, in the growth of *g* to *gv*, which combination has then become *b*: this is found both in Irish and the British languages ; fourthly, in the change of *j* into *dj* and then into *d*. This

---

[a] To No. 55 κῆλον çalja, add W. *col* 'peak,' 'sting,' Ir. *cuil* (gl. culex 'stachelbegabt,' Schmidt *die Wurzel AK*, 52), Guidel[2]. 57, W. *cylion* 'gnats.'
[b] In the nom. sg. masc. *int-ech* (e. g.) comes from *(s)ind-h-eco*, *sinda-s-ecvo-s*.

fourth change (the brilliant discovery of Mr. Rhys [a]) is, so far as I know, confined to Welsh, Cornish and Breton.

III.—NOTANDA.

I shall now mention some 38 Greek words which have apparently their cognates in the Celtic languages, but which, with three exceptions, are either not noticed in Curtius' book, or only referred to for non-comparative purposes :—

βρόγχος, O.Ir. *bráge* (gl. cervix), Z. 255, (an ant-stem), W. *breuant* 'windpipe;'

γοργών, γοργός, Ir. *garg* 'fierce,' Corm. Tr. 88, also *gearg* .i. *garg*, O'Cl.; γῦρος, Ir. *giugrann* (ex *gi-gur-ann*) 'anser bernicula,' Z. 21, Corm. Tr. 88, W. *gwyrain*;

ἐρείκη, (ἐ-Γρείκη), Ir. *froech*, gen. *froich*, Z. 918, W. *grug* 'heath ;' ἐρείκω, *rec* (gl. sulco), Z. 1063, (Mod. W. *rhyg* 'notch,' 'groove') : cf. ἤρεικον χθόνα ;

ἤϊθεος, root VADH 'heimführen,' 'heirathen,' Fick 179. O.Ir. root VOD in *in-bod-ugud* 'nubere,' *in-both-igetar* 'nubent,' Z. 1034, *in-botha* 'nuptias' (*th* for *dh*), Tur. 48, Corn. *d-om-eth-y*, BM. 327 = Br. *d-im-iz-iff* 'soy marier,' 'nubere ;'

ἤν, Lat. *en*, O.Ir. *énde*, Corm. Tr. 69, = O'Clery's *énne* .i. *féch no fionn* 'see or know !'

Ͽολός, Ͽολερός, Goth. *dval-s*, Eng. *dull*, = Ir. and W. *dall* 'blind,' Ir. *cluas-dall* 'deaf,' lit. 'ear-dull,' O'Cl., s.v. *athaile ;*

ἰσχνό-ς, ex σισκ-νος, W. *hesp* 'dry,' 'barren,' Ir. *sesc*, W. *hespin* 'a yearling ewe' = *seisc*, Corm., s.v. Oi. pl. *sesci* 'dry cows,' SM. ii. 120 ;

κέντρον, W. *cethr*, Ir. *cinteir* (gl. calcar), Z. 67, ex *cent-tri*. The O.Ir. *cét* 'a blow' (*col-dam aidid crist na cét* 'I know the death of Christ of the blows,' [b] Harl. 1802, fo. 9b) = O'Clery's *céad* .i. *béim*, is cognate with κεντέω, O.N. *hnjódha*, NHG. *nieten*, Fick 31, 730 ;

κέρκος 'cock, ' Hesych., Fick 35, Ir. *cerc* 'hen ;'

κίστρον, Ir. *casair* .i. *dealg* 'fibula,' *ceis* .i. *sleagh* 'hasta,' O'Cl. ;

κλάδος = *holz* (Fick, Spracheinheit, 310), Ir. *caill* 'sylva,' Z. 183,815, gen. *calle*, Fiacc's h. 16, but dat. *caillid* LL. 10. b. 2, a *t*-stem (*caldit*-), W. *celli ;*

κνήμη, Ir. *cnám* 'os,' nom. pl. *cnamai*, Z. 1003 ;

κρόμυον, Ir. *crem*, W. *craf* 'garlic ;'

λό-γ-χη, *la-n-cea*, O.Ir. *laigen ;*

---

[a] See *Revue Celtique* ii. 115, where Rhys equates *haidd* 'barley' ex *hahja* with Skr. *sasya;* *ardd-u* 'to plough' with Goth. *arj-an;* *Iwerddon* with *Iverjon(em)* ; *trydydd* for *tritija;* Skr. *trtiya* and *llonedd, caredd, chweroedd, gwyledd, llyfredd, mocledd, truedd, trugaredd* with the Irish fem. *yā*-stems *láine, caire, serbe, féle, lobre, máile, tróige, trúcaire.* The Welsh plurals in *edd* (Corn. *-eth*, Br. *-ez*) appear to have been originally collectives, identical in formation with Greek Ͽωρ-ιά, ἀνθρακ-ιά, μυρμηκ-ιά, νεοττ-ιά and Skr. *gav-yā* 'a number of cows,' Curtius' *Grundzüge* 595.

[b] See Matth. xxvii. 67 : Mark xv. 9. : Luke xxiii. 63, 64 : John xix. 3. In Dr. Reeves' edition of the *Codex Maelbrigte*, O'Curry renders *aidid crist nacét* by 'the fate of all-ruling Christ' ! *Aidid*, I think, always means 'death by violence.'

μαστός, 'a swelling breast,' Ir. *máss* 'buttock,' 'the bottom of a vessel' (*cen mas isin dabaig*, note to Fél. Nov. 24), also used in topography, as μαστός is used for a round hill or knoll; μάταιος = Ir. *madae*, Fél. Ep. 227, *in-madæ* (gl. sine causa), Z. 609; μί-μ-φ-υμαι (= *μεμέφομαι according to Pott), O.Ir. *mebul* 'shame,' Z. 711, W. *meflu* 'to disgrace;'

μικκός for μικ-*Γ*ος, Lat. *mac-ro-*, Old-Celt. *maqo-* 'filius,' Ir. *macc*, W. *map*; ὀθόνη, root VADH 'binden,' 'winden,' Fick 179. To this root, and not to BHADH, Windisch should have referred O. Ir. *co-beden* 'conjugatio,' *co-bod-las* 'conjunctio,' *coi-bd-elach* 'necessarius, amicus.' Had these words come from *bhadh*, they would have been *com-beden*, *com-bodlas*, *coim-bd-elach*. But they stand for *con-feden*, etc., as Ebel has seen, Z. 871, and the *b* is the graphic representative of *f* infected by the *n* of *con-*. Other derivatives from this VADH are: Ir. *fedan* 'jugum,' Corm. Tr. 79, W. *gwedd*, Ir. *fascud* (ex *vadcatu), Corm. Tr. 77, Br. *goascaff* 'stringere.'

οὐτάω, ὠτειλή, Ir. *futhu* 'stigmata,' *fothib* 'facibus,' *co-fothea-sa* (gl. ut mordeam), Z. 1005, Lith. *voti-s* 'wound;' πίτ-ρα, πίτ-ρος, Ir. *áith* 'fornax,' W. *od-yn*. So κάμινος and Skr. *açmanta* 'oven' are cognate with *açman* 'stone.' "Die ältesten öfen sind jedenfals steinerne herde oder in stein gehauene löcher gewesen, wie sie es zum teil bis auf den heutigen tag gebliben sind. Daher nante man sie auch 'steine'." Schmidt *Die Wurzel AK*, 66.

-πλοος, -πλους in ἁ-πλόος, διπλοῦς, Ir. *dia-bul*, *tri-pulta*, Ir.Gl. Nos. 930, 931;

ῥῦμα, O.W. *ruimmein* [a] (gl. vincula), Juv. 55: cf. NHG. *riemen*, Fick, *Spracheinheit* 359;

σκαμβός, Old-Celtic *cambo-*, Ir. *camm*, Z. 857, Br. *cam* 'boiteux;'

σπαργή, σπαργάω, (Skr. *sphurj*), W. *ffrau* 'torrent,' 'gushing.' That σπαργάω is connected with Lat. *turgeo* (Curtius 689) seems very doubtful;

ρητάω, O.Ir. *táid* 'thief,' *táin* 'cattle-spoil;' Τριτο(γένεια), etc., Ir. *triath* 'sea,' Corm. Tr. 156, *trethan* (gl. gurges), Z. 264, gen. *trethain* .i. *mara*, Fél. Nov. 23;

φυλλός = Ir. *ball* 'membrum,' Z. 222.

χάλιξ ex σκαλ-ιξ, O.Slav. *skala* 'stone,' Fick 408, Ir. *calad* 'hard,' O.W. *calet*, Ir. *cailte* .i. *cruas* 'hardness,' O'Cl.

χρέμπτομαι, χρέμψις ex *σκρε μ-π-τις (Lith. *skreplei*, Lat. *scrapta*, Fick 409), Ir. *crontaighim* 'I loathe, abhor, detest,' O'R., *crontaile* or *crointile* [b] 'pituita,' ex *scro-m-p-tal-ia*, as Br. *prount* ex *promptus*.

---

[a] The ms. has '*cuinhaunt irruimmein quæ det prena eterna super illos.*' Other such plurals are *cemmein* (gl. gradus), and *cnnein* = nomina, Mart. Cap. 11 a. a, 11 b. b. Rhys, Rev. Celt. ii. 119.

[b] The spellings *crontshaile, crointsheile* rest on one of Cormac's absurd etymologies, Corm. Tr. 36.

One might easily lengthen this list of wild Celtic words; but *boni venatoris est plures feras capere, non omnes.* I now present this paper to Windisch in hopes that he will criticise my work as freely as I have criticised his, that he will choose from my citations what seems to him worthy of Curtius' admirable book, and that he will pardon my presumption because of my strong desire that nothing unsound should be added to that book, and that no unsteady superstructure should be raised on the foundation so well and truly laid by Zeuss and Ebel.

CALCUTTA, *June 1st*, 1874.   W. S.

ADDENDA.

No. 2.   *Cem-ec-id* (gl. lapidaria), Z. 1061, = Mod.-W. *cyf-eg-ydd* 'pick-axe.'

No. 7.   Root ἀλκ, ἀρκ.   Add O.Ir. *timm-urc* 'coarcto,' Z. 979 ; *du-imm-airethe* (gl. artabatur), Z. 884 ; *tess-urc* 'defendo,' 'servo ;' *du-m-es-urc-sa*, Z. 881, 949, 953n ; *do-nn-es-airefe* 'nos servabit,' Goidel². 133.

No. 85.   Root λακ.   In O.Ir *at-luchur*, *dutt-luchur*, Z. 438, the *-luchur* is identical in root and meaning with Lat. *loquor.* The root-vowel *a* appears in the conjunctive *tod-laiger-sa* (gl. postolem), Ml. 38c.

No. 216.   With the στηνο in ἐύ(σ)-στηνος I would put the *-san* in O.Ir. *cum-sanad* 'quies,' Z. 872, and *to-san* 'station (?)' Rev. Celt. i. 67.

No. 231.   Root ταк.   Add O.Ir. *ro-tachatar* (fugerunt), Ml. 44a ; *arateget* (quia fugiunt), Ml. 48d ; *in-tech* 'path,' Goidel². 155.

No. 235.   Root ρεк.   The O.Ir. *techtaim* 'habeo' may be compared in form with τίκτω, in meaning with OHG. *digju*. The infinitive *conutecht* (*con-od-tech-t*, Ml. 139c, Goidel². 29) seems to belong to this root.

No. 507.   From the root *vart* here cited comes the O.Ir. verb *ad-bart-aigim̃* (for *advartaigim̃*) 'adverso,' of which many forms are cited by M. Nigra, Rev. Celt. i. 152.

CORRIGENDA.

p. 1, l. 16, for '*cobeden*' read '*olann, fual* ;'

p. 6, No. 37, omit the last line ;

p. 14, No. 178, omit the last two sentences ;

p. 20, No. 325, omit the second sentence : *indib* is nothing but ' visceribus,' ' medullis ;'

p. 31, No. 658, l. 2, *for* 'I think with' *read* 'according to' and *before* ' cf.' *insert* ' but.'

GOIDELICA, SECOND EDITION.

Corrigenda.

[*Vide supra,* p. 6, note.]

Pref., line 3, *for* ' codex ' *read* 'Berne, Leyden and Carinthian Codices ;' .
p. 7, gl. 58, *for* ' pray' *read* ' utter thanks ;' gl. 65, *for* ' seas' *read* ' waters ;'
p. 9, gl. 87, *for* ' decoration' *read* ' robe ;'
p. 12, gl. 118, *for* ' he offended it' *read* ' it denied him' *(dodrolluind=do-d-ro-sluind),* Ebel, Z. 874 ; gl. 127a, *read* ' tacmungad nadbran(n co . . .)
—which surrounded *(him)* from ankle to . . . ;' gl. 128 *for* . . . . *read*
' a kid (?) ', and with *innaric* cf. O.W. *enderic,* Beitr. vii. 411.
p. 13, gl. 138, *for* ' cornered' *read* ' quartered ;'
p. 14, note, *for* ' kindles' *read* ' warms ;'
p. 16, l. 16, *for* ' goraim' *read* ' guirim ;'
p. 19, n. 26, *for* ' apparent *(batoich = baddoich)*' *read* ' meet *(batoich*
' conveniebat,' Z. 639) ;' n. 34, correct by reference to pp. 86, 91 ; n. 41,
for ' to be naked' *read* ' it be night.' (If we may read *cesu nocht is*
aldu de, translate ' quamvis sit nox est pulchrior eo ') ; n. 42, *for* ' he
would not get' *read* ' there showers not even ;'
p. 24, l. 18 from bottom, *for* ' road' *read* ' field ;'
p. 29, n. 34r, *for* ' life' *read* ' soul ;'
p. 29, n. 30r, *read* ' they deign not to inflict (?) upon them (any) other death
but striking,' &c.
p. 31, l. 16 from bottom, *for* ' the breast of a virgin' *read* ' a virgin's breasts ;'
p. 32, 18c, *read* ' conai[r]lemmarni ;'
p. 33, 19d, *for* ' est' *read* ' erat ;' 20a, *read* ' donai[d]bset ;'
p. 34, l. 4, *for* ' debebant' *read* ' debuerunt ;'
p. 37, 34d, *after* ' doirethi' *insert* ' [leg. dóirthi ?] ;'
p. 38, l. 11, for ' consumpsit' *read* ' consumptus est ; ' l. 5 from bottom, *for*
' forrarsissiu' *read* ' forrassissiu ;'
p. 39, l. 29, *for* ' (leg. artatar ?) ' *read* ' i. e., coarctatus sum.'
p. 66, l. 28, *after* ' furnus' *insert* ' frenum ;'
p. 90, l. 14, *for* ' family' *read* ' province,' and correct Z². 639, l. 5, accordingly ;
p. 102, l. 12 from bottom, *for* ' there ' *read* ' three ;'
p. 129, l. 8, *for* ' imlobor' *read* ' indlobor ;'
p. 129, l. 5 from bottom, *for* ' with his circuit' *read* ' to sojourn with him ; '
p. 130, l. 8, *for* ' at Sletty in the North-West' *read* ' to the North-West of
Sletty ;'
p. 131, note e, *for* ' jati' *read* ' gati ;'
p. 133, l. 16 from bottom, *for* ' will . . . shall' *read* ' would . . . should ;
l. 3 of the hymn, read ' not much of carping was found (in her): with
the noble faith of the Trinity (she lived) ;'
p. 142, hymn, l. 10, *read* ' a town sheltered her : when she went (thence)
it protected hosts ;'

p. 113, hymn, l. 25, *for* 'calling' *read* 'herding ;' l. 26, *for* 'food' *read* 'stock ;' l. 27, *for* 'marvel' *read* 'triumph ;' l. 30, *read* 'there was dry weather till night ᵃ in her field, though throughout the world it poured with rain ;' l. 33, *for* 'storm' *read* 'rain ;'

p. 144, hymn, lines 51, 56 *for* 'sent' and 'helped' *read* 'directed ;'

p. 145, l. 19, *for* 'dwelt (?)' *read* 'refreshed her ;' note d, *read* 'argenteum .... mare ;'

p. 146, l. 13, *for* 'serca' *read* 'sancta ;'

p. 149, l. 1, *for* 'me' *read* 'us ;' l. 12, *for* 'love thou the sage,' *read* 'holy sage,' (*sruith*, like *flaith*, is feminine, though applied to a male) ;

p. 159, the first quatrain should follow the second, and l. 4 should run on with the last line of p. 158 ;

p. 175, l. 2, *for* '501' *read* '101 ;'

p. 179, note 21, l. 4, *for* 'airshetal' *read* 'airchetal ;'

p. 181, last l., *for* 'a shrine which gold accompanies' *read* 'a holy shrine which gold bedecks ;' and with *con-u-taing* cf. *co-ta-u-taing* 'eam protegit,' Ml. 36b. Have we here a nasalised form of the root (*s*)*tag*, No. 155, to be compared with στεγνός, στεγνόω ?

p. 182, l. 12, *for* 'an *udnacht*' *read* 'a palisade ;'

See also M. Nigra's corrections of pp. 23—51, in the *Revue Celtique* i. 505, 506, and Prof. Windisch's in the *Literarisches Centralblatt*, 15 März, 1873.

p. 20, line 14, *for* 'boy' *read* 'Son :' *for* 'a man' *read* 'his Father ;' and note that the idea of a miraculous parturition by a male may have been suggested by S. Paul : 'Filioli mei, quos iterum parturio' (Galat. iv. 19) ; 'Etenim in Christo Jesu per evangelium ego vos genui' (1 Corinth. iv. 15). In the Lebar Brecc, p. 74, col. 4, Christ is thus addressed : *A mic roghenair fodíi* ('O Son, who wast born twice !') ; and in the same page, col. 2 : *A mic ind-athar aircisectaig cin máthair anim* ('O Son of the merciful Father, without a mother in heaven !') ; *A mic ina fire oigi muire ingine cin athair italam* ('O Son of the true Virgin Mary, the maiden, without a father on earth !').

In p. 148, the following translation of the Irish part of the preface to Sanctáin's hymn was accidentally omitted :—

"'*I beseech the King.*'—Bishop Sanctain made this hymn, and when he was going from Clonard westward to Matóc's Island ᵇ he made it. And he was a brother of Matóc's, and both of them were of Britain, and Matóc came into Ireland before Bishop Sanctain. Now the *causa* is this : to save him(self) from enemies, and that his brother might be let come *in insulam* to him. *Scoticam*, etc."

ᵃ *coidchi*, O'Clery's *chaidche* .i. *go hoidhche. amhail adeir an muimhneach* ('as saith the Munsterman') *cá rabhadhais la choidhche* .i. *ca hionadh ina rabadhais ar feidh an láoi gonuige an oidhche* ('in what place hast thou been throughout the day until the night ?')
ᵇ An islet in the lake of Templeport, country Leitrim. O'Curry's *Lectures on the MS. Materials of Ancient Irish History*, p. 27, and see Z. præf. xiii and Rel. Celt. 21.

The latter part of the story of the Devil and S. Molling at pp. 180, 181 is very badly rendered. It should run thus:—

'Wherefore hast thou come?' asked Molling.

'That thou mayst give me thy blessing,' says the Devil.

'I will not give it,' says Molling. 'Since thou deservest [a] it not, thou wouldst not be the better thereof. What good were it to thee moreover?'

'O Cleric,' says he, 'just as if thou shouldst go into a vat of honey and bathe therein with thy raiment, the odour thereof would be on thee unless thy raiment should be washen [b].'

'Wherefore is this thy desire?' asks Molling.

'Because, though thou givest nought of thy blessing to me, the benefit and goodness thereof will be on me externally.'

'Thou shall not have it,' says Molling, 'for thou deservest [a] it not.'

'Well then,' says he, 'give me the full of a curse.'

'Wherefore wishest thou this?' says Molling.

'Not hard to say, O Cleric,' says he: 'on thy mouth will (then) be the venom and hurt of every mouth whereon gathers [c] the curse on me.'

'Go,' says Molling, 'to no blessing hast thou a right.'

'Better were it for me that I should have a right to it. How shall I attain it?'

'By service unto God,' says Molling.

'Woe's me,' says he, 'I render not this.'

'A ... reading (of holy texts),' says Molling.

'Thy reading saves me not [d], and this does not help me.'

'Fasting then,' says Molling.

'I am fasting since the world's beginning. Not the better am I.'

'Making genuflexions,' says Molling.

'I cannot bend forward, for my knees are (turned) backward.'

'Go forth,' says Molling, 'I cannot save thee.'

Then said the Devil, '*He is pure gold*,' etc.

---

[a] -*airle* for *airilli*: cf. *naichid airilset* (gl. non promerentibus), Ml. 51, *airilliud* 'meritum,' Z. 802.

[b] *nestá* 3d sg. secondary s-fut. passive of *nigim*.

[c] *targa* cf. *tárgadh* .i. *tionol no cruinninghadh*, O'Cl.

[d] *ni-m-ó* for *ní-mm-ói* v. supra, note on No. 586.

LIST OF ABBREVIATIONS.

A.S. Anglo-Saxon.

Beitr. *Beiträge zur vergleichenden sprachforschung*, vols. i—vii.

BM. *Beunans Meriasek*, a Cornish Drama, London, 1872.

Br. Breton.

Brocc. h. *Broccán's hymn*, printed in *Goidelica*, pp. 137—140.

Cath. *The Catholicon of Lagadeuc*, ed. Le Men.

Colm. h. *Colmán's hymn*, printed in *Goidelica*, pp. 121—123.

Corm. *Cormac's Glossary*, printed in *Three Irish Glossaries*, London, 1862.

Corm. Tr. *Cormac's Glossary*, translated by O'Donovan, Calcutta, 1868.

Fél. *Félire Oengusso*, in *Lebar Brecc*, pp. 75--106.

Fiacc's h. *Fiacc's hymn*, printed in *Goidelica*, pp. 126—128.

Fick. *Vergleichendes Wörterbuch der indogermanischen sprachen*, 1870.

Glück KN. Glück's *Die bei Caius Julius Cæsar vorkommenden keltischen namen*, München, 1857.

Goidel. *Goidelica*, London, Trübner & Co., 1872.

H. 2. 16.
H. 3. 18. } MSS. in the library of Trinity College, Dublin.

Ir. Gl. *Irish Glosses*, Dublin, 1860.

Juv. *Codex Juvenci Cantabrigiensis*, Beitr. iv. 385, vii. 410.

LB. *Lebar Brecc*, a 15th century MS. in the library of the Royal Irish Academy.

Lhuyd A.B. Lhuyd's *Archæologia Britannica*, 1707.

Lib. Arm. *Liber Armachanus*, a 9th century MS. in the library of Trinity College, Dublin.

Lith. Lithuanian.

LL. *Book of Leinster*, a 12th century MS. in the library of Trinity College, Dublin.

LU. *Lebar na huidre*, a 12th century MS. in the library of the Royal Irish Academy.

M.Br. Middle-Breton.

Ml. *Codex Mediolanensis*, Bibl. Ambros., C. 301.

NHG. Modern High German.

O'Cl. *O'Clery's Glossary*, Louvain, 1643.

O'Dav. *O'Davoren's Glossary*, printed in *Three Irish Glossaries*, pp. 47—124.

O'Don. Gr. O'Donovan's *Grammar of the Irish Language*, Dublin, 1845.

O'Don. Supp. O'Donovan's *Supplement to O'Reilly's Dictionary*.

OHG. Old High German. **O.Ir.** Old Irish. **O.N.** Old Norse.

O'R. O'Reilly's *Irish-English Dictionary*, 1821.

O.Sax. Old Saxon. **O.W.** Old Welsh.

P. *The Passion*, a Middle-Cornish poem, Asher, Berlin, 1862.

Rel. Celt. *Reliquiæ Celticæ*, ed. Nigra, 1872.

Rev. Celt. *Revue Celtique*, ed. Gaidoz.

Sg. *Prisciani Codex Sancti Galli*, in Z. and Rel. Celt.

SM. *Senchas Mór*, vol. i, Dublin, 1865; vol. ii, Dublin, 1869; vol. iii, Dublin, 1873.

Tur. *The Turin Glosses*, Goidel., pp. 3—13.

W. Welsh.

Z. Zeuss' *Grammatica Celtica*, ed. Ebel, 1871.

www.ingramcontent.com/pod-product-compliance
Lightning Source LLC
Chambersburg PA
CBHW021443090426
42739CB00009B/1624